JAMES MAY'S
MAN LAB

Also by James May
*James May's Magnificent Machines, James May's 20th Century,
Car Fever, How to Land an A330 Airbus*

JAMES MAY'S
MAN LAB
THE BOOK OF USEFULNESS

James May and Will Maclean

Illustrations by
Simon Ecob and Alex Morris

HODDER

The Authors

James May is a writer, broadcaster and co-host of *Top Gear* on BBC2. He writes a weekly column in the *Daily Telegraph* and has presented series for the BBC, ITV, Channel 4 and Sky.

Will Maclean was born and brought up in Merseyside, but now lives in London. He has written professionally for seven years, and amateurishly for many years before that. He's written material for a variety of television shows. Most valued manskill: reglazing windows.

The Illustrators

Simon Ecob has worked as a freelance cartoonist and illustrator for the last twenty years. He enjoyed a long association with *Viz* Comic where, as well as producing numerous paintings and illustrated features, he was principal artist on the strip *Jack Black*. His comic work has also appeared in *Spectacular Spider-Man* and *Cosmic* magazine. He has illustrated a variety of children's books, including the *The Unbeatable Boys' Book*, *The Boys' Book of Survival* and *Disgusting Jokes for Kids*.

Alex Morris is one of the designers and creators of the bestselling books *The Framley Examiner* and *Bollocks to Alton Towers* as well as being a regular contributor to *Viz* Comic. He can also fix a leaking tap, repair a hoover and construct garden decking, but somehow managed to completely knacker the back wheel on his daughter's bicycle whilst trying to repair it. Sorry, Daisy.

Contents

Introduction

You are holding in your hands the book of usefulness. We're not claiming that this is the definitive reference work on being useful, because that would be a very big book indeed, and would have to include instructions on playing the Theremin and building your own lunar lander.

Instead, this volume, densely packed with useful information and guidance though it is, should be thought of more as usefulness's muse; the inspiration to have a go at some art or craft skill you imagined to be beyond you, and reassuring confirmation that it's OK to be excited by chisels.

This is what *Man Lab* is all about – having a go at something that seems like a good idea, even if it turns out not to be. The Man Lab ethos is probably best represented by our Swiss Army Bicycle.

It occurred to us, in our home-made bar, that the bicycle as we know it, has been with us since 1885,

when John Kemp Starley designed and built his 'Rover Safety Bicycle'. But for all that time it has rested rather arrogantly on its laurels. Certainly, the basic idea has been refined considerably, but a bicycle is still only a bicycle, and suitable only for riding around on.

Interestingly, just a few years after that seminal bicycle another man, named Karl Elsener, gave us the first of what would come to be known as the Swiss Army Penknife. He successfully added a second blade to the previously single-bladed clasp knife, and from there he and his followers went on to add the tin opener, the corkscrew, the tweezers, and everything else we like to have in our pockets. Today, a dazzling range of these knives is available, tailored to the needs of anglers, campers, rescue teams and even watch repairers.

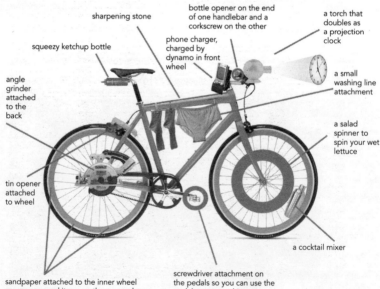

sharpening stone

bottle opener on the end of one handlebar and a corkscrew on the other

a torch that doubles as a projection clock

squeezy ketchup bottle

phone charger, charged by dynamo in front wheel

angle grinder attached to the back

a small washing line attachment

a salad spinner to spin your wet lettuce

tin opener attached to wheel

a cocktail mixer

sandpaper attached to the inner wheel so you can sand items on the go or when the bike is upside down

screwdriver attachment on the pedals so you can use the pedal as a screwdriver

The Swisss Army Bicycle – an early prototype.

This is the thinking we applied to our bike, and arrived at the Swiss Army Bicycle Village Handyman Edition. It's still a bicycle, but it is also equipped to allow its rider to clean windows, attach hinges, creosote fences, sharpen knives, repair other bicycles and prepare delicious fruit-based milky beverages. With this as a template, surely other bespoke multi-tool bicycles will follow.

Sadly, the Swiss Army Bike came to us some time after the contents of this book had been prepared for print, and therefore does not appear in the following pages. So this introduction has not really been very useful at all. Maybe next time. Meanwhile, here is another picture.

The Swiss Army Bicycle Village Handyman Edition – the dawn of a new age of usefulness for men.

Man Lab Floor Plan

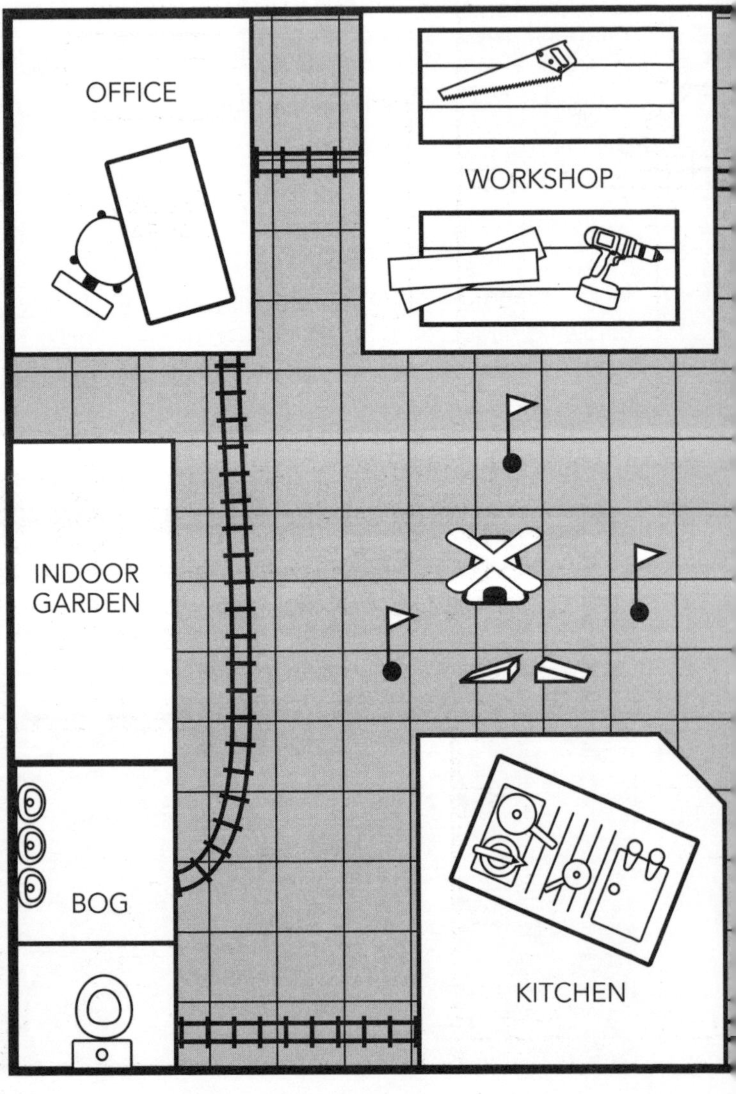

OFFICE

WORKSHOP

INDOOR GARDEN

BOG

KITCHEN

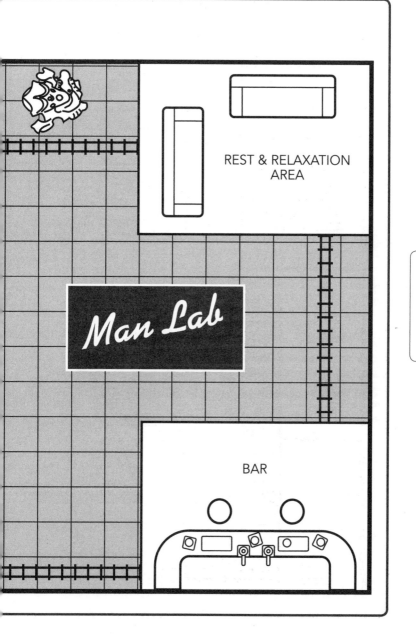

REST & RELAXATION
AREA

Man Lab

BAR

Welcome to the Man Lab! A place where men will rediscover their practical, creative sides and re-acquaint themselves with skills and knowledge they thought long-lost. Skills such as how to drive a spile into a cask of ale, and knowing what a 'spile' is in the first place.

It's here where we will arrest the decline of the modern male, and turn him from a moisturising, sandal-wearing blob of jelly in an ironic T-shirt into the dependable, knowledgeable sort of bloke who knows how to put up a shelf, woo a lady, and punch a lion.* Remember – this is our Man Lab, and yours will be different. But the same ethos, and the same spirit of curiosity and can-do, will pervade it.

WORKSHOP
A plywood playroom, where most of the Man Lab toolkit is, and also the home of the Man Lab cement mixer, which comes in abnormally handy for all manner of stuff. If you don't possess a toolkit, fear not – we have full and frank instructions on how to assemble a basic one throughout the book.

TOOLS ON SHADOW BOARD
Nothing says 'I have a full toolkit and what is more I am taking proper care of it' like a good old-fashioned shadow board. Not only are your tools sharpened up, stored properly out of harm's way and ready for use, you also know at a glance if someone called Colin has borrowed one and not put it back. (It's the 10mm spanner.)

REST & RELAXATION AREA
Two sofas – an essential for any self-respecting man-space – facing a coffee table. (Despite what the style sections of men's magazines will tell you, a coffee table need be no more than a sheet of plywood on four paint cans, and can be used to serve tea.) Also has shelves full of strange and weird nick-nacks and toys, to encourage creative thought and productive arsing about.

KITCHEN
This contains the concrete kitchen worktop. Hewn from proper man-sweat (and also a lot of concrete), designed by the finest engineering brains in modern Britain, this heavy-duty work surface is lovingly crafted to provide us with everything we need in terms of a modern kitchen sink unit. You can find out how to make your own elsewhere in the book.

INTEGRATED RAILWAY SYSTEM
The very lifeblood of the Man Lab complex. This – perhaps the only properly functioning railway system left in the UK – ferries important items hither and yon, from the kitchen to the office and all points in-between. Need a banana?

* Probably not the last one.

Can't actually be bothered getting up to get one? Just summon the Man Lab Express. This really is an engineering marvel – it even includes a pneumatic railway bridge spanning the doorway between the bog and the rest of the building. We'll be going into more detail about this later.

BAR

Distressed at the decline of the British pub, we fought back and built our very own Man Lab bar, a bespoke blokes' hang-out where foaming nut-brown ale is always on tap, and the last orders bell never rings. (In fact, we don't even have a last orders bell, just to be on the safe side.) It's here that we unwind after a hard day spent re-skilling the male population of the world. Needless to say, this volume contains full instructions on how to equip your own bar.

BOG

Perhaps the only convenience in the world to be fitted with a device that tells you when the bog-roll is about to run out. This futuristic marvel represents the greatest advancement in bog technology since Thomas Crapper patented the ballcock.

INDOOR GARDEN

In the aftermath of a nuclear war, we'd probably be OK for courgettes, thanks to the presence of the Man Lab indoor garden – an 'optimum condition outdoor simulation environment' in which all manner of fruit and veg can be grown, and grown all year round. No longer is indoor gardening the preserve of weirdos, or students attempting to grow free 'jazz cigarettes'.

STATUE OF GANESH

Ganesh, or Ganesha, is the elephant-headed Hindu god of removing obstructions or obstacles. Ironically, there was a large stone Ganesh in the Man Lab when we took it over, and it's too heavy to move. This is the original 'elephant in the room'.

CRAZY GOLF HOLES

But it's not all work, work, work. After a hard day knocking rawls into walls, why not relax by knocking balls into holes? You can if you've rigged up some Crazy Golf holes in your Man Lab. Having a Crazy Golf course at home means you don't have to pay a fiver to a grubby man in a kiosk on a windswept beachfront in order to play this ancient and noble sport – you can simply tee up at your leisure. 90% more fun than proper golf or your money back.

This, then, is our Man Lab – our base of operations from which we'll re-skill the Modern Man. Anyway, enough shilly-shallying – let's get excited and do stuff. What shall we kick off with? Ah yes. I know.

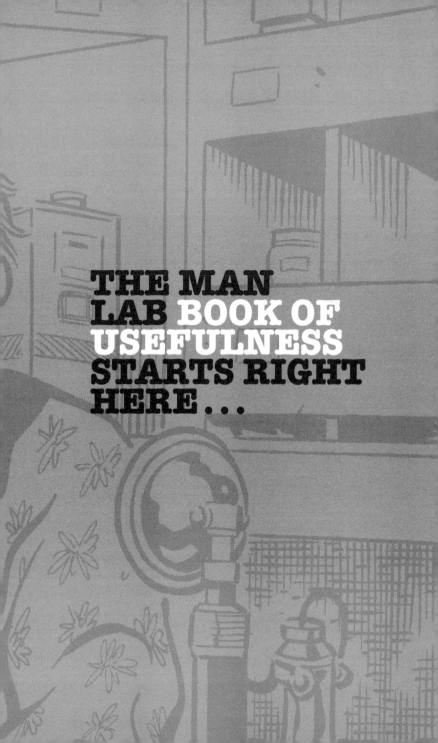

THE MAN LAB BOOK OF USEFULNESS STARTS RIGHT HERE . . .

TAKING PENALTIES

Has there ever been a bigger affront to English national pride than the humiliation of a penalty shoot-out? At least *It's a Royal Knockout* is something that is slowly fading from living memory, whereas the penalty shoot-out is the humiliation that just keeps on giving. Those three little words – 'penalty shoot-out' – are guaranteed to strike fear into the core of any right-thinking Englishman, as they recall the shame and horror of the 1990 World Cup. And Euro '96. And the 1998 World Cup. And the 2004 European Championships. And the 2006 World Cup.

In fact, it's pretty much a given that whenever we're forced to take penalties, the England squad might as well head off for an early bath. But is it really that hard? I mean, it's only kicking a ball into a goal, for God's sake – the one thing they're paid fifty grand a week to do.

And so I went to investigate.

'A penalty is a cowardly way to score' – PELÉ

The problem

The bare facts of this particular problem, as far as I can see it, are as follows:

England have proven themselves pretty useless at taking penalties. The thing is, saying England are 'pretty useless' at penalty shoot-outs is a major understatement. To be blunt about it, we are dreadful. Awful. Execrable. So bad, in fact, that we're officially the worst at penalty-taking among the world's top seventy teams in major finals.

That's right – the actual worst. No other team has a history of shame that beats our miserable international record: played 7, won 1, lost 6. This amounts to a 14% success rate – and to put that into some sort of perspective, that's worse than Swaziland or the Maldives. Or Belgium. In fact, if all the world's football teams were forced to have their penalty-taking abilities represented by actual people, England would be a slovenly middle-aged bloke with bad hair and oddly shaped feet who gets picked last for five-a-side. Me, in fact.

The really galling thing about all of this is that – as our German friends keep demonstrating, over and over again, as if to rub it in – taking a penalty is really rather easy.

Kicking off (sorry)

Thus, my mission was a simple one. To discover (if possible) a foolproof method by which the England squad could take penalties, thus overcoming their fear of the shoot-out; thus allowing them to win more matches; thus restoring national pride and once again making sure the English male could carry himself with his head held high; thus ushering in a new 'golden age' for football.

As I say – simple.

The basics

As far as I, a neutral observer, could see, the aim of a penalty kick was as follows:

1. Kick ball past 'goalkeeper' into 'goal', thus 'scoring' 'a goal'.
2. THAT'S IT.

I checked my facts twice to make sure I hadn't missed something. But no – there didn't seem to be anything more to it than that.

However, after I'd been looking into it for a while, I began to see that the matter was much more complicated than I'd first suspected. Possibly more complicated than the human brain could comprehend.

Penalty science

Because England have been so consistently bad at taking penalties, and because this has cost us dear both financially and in terms of national esteem, a massive amount of money has been spent researching the science behind penalty kicks.

For instance: Loughborough University's Sports Tech department has even created its own robot striker, to show the flesh-and-blood players how it's done. 'David', as he's known, is capable of kicking balls for 100 metres at speeds of up to 100 mph, and what's more he can perform the same stunningly accurate kicks over and over again. David's owner, Dr Andy Harland, says of his striker automaton, rather confusingly, 'It's way more capable than any player; it just doesn't have a brain.' Sadly, being a robot means that David is ineligible for the England squad – and as he also helped design the balls for the last two World Cups, it can be argued that David's done us no favours at all.

The Magic Formula – 1

In 2006, a news story did the rounds that ran thus: Scientific research into the art of taking penalties had been done by the good people at Liverpool John Moores University, and they were so proud of their findings they sent them to then England boss Sven Goran-Eriksson (a man who certainly knew a thing or two about scoring).

The story went on to describe how scientists at John Moores arrived at their findings. Firstly, they looked at, and analysed, all of England's penalties since 1962. Then, they broke down the action of taking a penalty into the following, easy-to-understand equation:

$$(((X+Y+S)/2)x((T+I+2B)/4))+(V/2)-1$$

As it stands, this is gibberish, even in the mind of Wayne Rooney. But it starts to make a bit more sense when you know what those letters stand for:

V = Velocity of ball once struck
T = Time between placing ball on spot and striking ball
S = Number of steps in run-up
I = Time ball is struck after goalkeeper initiates dive
Y = Vertical placement of ball from ground
X = Horizontal placement of ball from centre
B =Striking position of foot

The newspapers who reported this story explained that, in order to make this formula work for us, we had to do the following:

Add **X** (the horizontal placement of ball from the centre of the goal) to **Y** (the vertical placement of the ball from the ground) and then add **S** (being the number of steps in the run-up). Divide this by two then multiply this result by: the sum of **T** (the time between placing ball on spot and striking the ball) and **I** (the time the ball is struck after goalkeeper initiates dive) plus two times **B** (the striking position of foot). Now divide this by four. Now add **V** (the Velocity of the ball once struck) divided by two.

Finally take away 1 from the final result and voila! You have scored a penalty. And probably simultaneously passed your maths A-Level.

The big problem with this equation is, of course, that you can't expect anyone whose job isn't to study the science of penalty kicks to apply it to actually taking a penalty (although maybe David Beckham was mentally trying to do this when he took his famously bad penalty during Euro 2004).

Now, the more mathematically-minded among you might have noticed that the formula isn't even a formula as such. Furthermore, when it came to research this story for the Man Lab book you now hold in your hands, we discovered that this story was shrouded in mystery – numerous phone calls to Liverpool John Moores, plus our own research couldn't locate the author, a Dr David Lewis. So, Dr Lewis – if you're out there – please get in touch, and explain your findings to us in greater detail. Your country needs you. (Unless you're Welsh, in which case your interest in the fortunes of the England football team is probably not great.)

The findings

Confusingly, however, Professor Tim Cable – the Director of Sport and Exercise Science at Liverpool John Moores, and a man whom we did manage to locate – also undertook some research into the science of taking penalties, and his investigation led to some useful findings. Professor Cable discovered that:

- The ideal velocity for the ball is 25–29 metres per second (65 mph), and the ideal number of steps in a run-up to be four to six. A long run-up of 10 m is the least successful.
- The best angle to approach the ball at is 20–30 degrees.
- The best place in the goalmouth to place the ball and ensure a goal is 50 cm below the crossbar and 50 cm from inside the post.

Therefore, if you take four to six steps run–up, kick the ball at 25 to 29 metres per second, approaching the ball at an angle of 20 to 30 degrees while making sure that you kick the ball at no less than 50 cm below the crossbar and no less than 50 cm from inside the post – you WILL score a penalty.

The Magic Formula – 2

Unsurprisingly, Professor Cable wasn't the only person to attempt to boil down penalty-taking to a foolproof method. Nick Morgan and a team of sports scientists working for Lucozade Sport also analysed thousands of successful penalties and their takers, and they came up with the following, long (but actually workable) formula:

$$lps = \frac{1(rf)+1(s/d)+1(a=21)+1(t<45)}{4} + \frac{1(opb)+1(sru)+1(ns)+1(ib)+1(tlc)}{5}$$

Once again, this looks more complex than it is. Basically, 'lps' on the left-hand side stands for 'likely penalty success', while the right-hand side of the equation is divided into two sections, the first of which is all about the player, and the second is all about how to take the kick. The result will give you your personal likelihood of scoring.

Which means you can work out how likely you are to score by breaking down the equation into its component parts, and answering a series of yes/no questions.

Let's do that.

How likely are you to score a penalty?

Are you right-footed? (rf)
Yes: 1 No: 0
(This is important because right-footers apparently score 71% of their penalties compared to 52% of lefties.)

Are you a striker or a defender? (s/d)
Striker: 1 Defender: 0
(Defenders miss more penalties than strikers. For the record, attacking players successfully convert 83.1% of their penalties, midfield players convert 79.6% and defenders convert a measly 73.6%.)

Are you 21 or under? (a=21)
Yes: 1 No: 0

(Younger penalty-takers are more successful than older teammates. Players aged 22 or younger successfully convert 85.2% of attempts. Those aged between 23 and 28 convert 77.6%, and those aged over 29 years convert 78.1%.)

Have you been on the pitch less than 45 minutes? (t<45)
Yes: 1 No: 0

(You're more likely to score if you're not knackered.)

So much for the 'player' side of the equation. Now for 'technique':

Do you start your run outside the penalty box? (opb)
Yes: 1 No: 0

Do you take a slow run-up? (sru)
Yes: 1 No: 0

(A slow, measured run-up is more likely to succeed.)

Will you be kicking across the keeper to the left side, or nearside, of the goal? (ns)
Yes: 1 No: 0

(This is the most natural way to kick right-footed.)

Will you be side-footing it (i.e. kicking it with the inside of your boot)? (ib)
Yes: 1 No: 0

Finally:

Top left-hand corner? (tlc)
Yes: 1 No: 0

Now – divide the player scores by four. Next, divide the technique score by five. Add the two together, and divide by two.
Times this number by 100 to give you your percentage likelihood of scoring. Simple!

Armed with these two studies, we're now making real headway towards achieving the perfect penalty. But there are factors involved in penalty-taking that no amount of maths can help you with – namely the pressure, the crowd . . . and the opposing team's goalie.

> **TIP:** Don't try and 'trick' the goalie. This breaks the flow of the moment and increases your chances of failure.

Psychological warfare

'In football everything is complicated by the presence of the other team' – JEAN-PAUL SARTRE

Of course, if the formula was all there was to it, taking a penalty would be relatively plain sailing. But you're not the only person involved in this ritual; no sir. You have to knock the ball past the goalkeeper, and he will be doing his utmost to put you off, either by staring you out, acting the fool, or dancing around like a crab with a weak bladder. Not only that, if you're showing off your penalty-taking skills somewhere where they genuinely will make a difference to the nation – Wembley Stadium, say – there'll doubtless be a large crowd of people watching who do not want you to succeed, and won't be shy about expressing this opinion.

> **TIP:** Try and anticipate the keeper's dive. Wait for the keeper to start moving (usually a whole 0.31–0.4 milliseconds before striking the ball). Don't wait too long though – any longer than 0.41 milliseconds and the chances of scoring are halved.

Sports psychologists advise that the best way to deal with all of this pressure – the crowd, the goalie, even the expectations of your teammates – is to simply blot it all out, difficult as that sounds. (Some experts even maintain that increased awareness of the situation increases the likelihood of failure, and stress the importance of trying not to over-think what you're doing.)

Clarity and focus are the key qualities you will need to remain calm and take a successful penalty.

> **TIP:** Employ positive visualisation, as recommended by management training gurus. Try and visualise where the ball will go and it landing there flawlessly. Rehearse this skill in practice so that it becomes instinctive, rather than a conscious effort.

Taking a penalty: once and for all

'Behind every kick of the ball there has to be a thought'
— DENNIS BERGKAMP

Distilled from the methods devised by our greatest sporting brains, and years of bitter experience, here is the definitive Man Lab guide to penalty taking, in ten easy-to-remember steps.

1. PLACE THE BALL PROPERLY
Always do this yourself. Twist the ball back 30 degrees, to make it 'sit up' on the turf. You don't want some minor kink in the field to ruin your chances. Take your time doing it – research indicates that players who took longer placing the ball on the spot were more likely to score. Though you shouldn't take forever doing it either.

2. GET YOUR RUN-UP RIGHT
Remember: 4–6 paces are best – any more and you give too much of your intentions away to the goalie; any less and you can't build up the power required to hammer the ball home.

> **TIP:** Aim just inside either post, either high to the top or low to the bottom. Anything mid-height gives the goalkeeper the best chance of making a save.

3. PLANT YOUR STANDING FOOT FIRMLY AND WELL

Where you position your standing foot is crucial – you should do it so that the knee of the leg you take the kick with is over the ball. This will enable you to take the most accurate shot possible. This is another thing worth practising until it becomes instinctive.

4. GIVE THOUGHT TO HOW YOU KICK THE BALL

Power and accuracy are two different things, and come from different parts of the foot, so think about how you're going to achieve your kick. Remember – anything faster than 30 metres per second enhances the risk of a miss because of the loss in accuracy.

5. CHOOSE WHERE TO KICK THE BALL LONG BEFORE YOU START THE RUN-UP

See also Step 9 (Disguise your body shape).

6. OUT-PSYCH THE KEEPER

Try at the very least to show you're not bothered by him and his wacky antics, and appear confident and relaxed. Don't be tempted to trick the goalie – it will reduce your chances of success and could easily backfire. A study by the University of Exeter concluded that players who ignored the goalkeeper and focused on where they wanted to shoot improved their accuracy (do universities do nothing but study penalty-taking?).

7. THINK (BRIEFLY) BEFORE YOU KICK

Research has shown that players who took less than 200 milliseconds to respond to the whistle scored less than 57% of the time on average, while players who took over a second to react scored just over 80% of the time on average. The message is clear – don't just whack the ball on the Pavlovian signal of the ref's whistle – think about what you're doing.

8. VISUALISE THE BALL GOING IN

A positive mental attitude and a complete understanding of what you want to achieve are the foundations for a successful penalty, whereas uncertainty over what you're about to do will seriously damage your chances of scoring. Don't consider your potential failure; imagine your success. Your attitude is your targeting system, and will help you to dent the net when it counts most.

TIP: Taking too long to take a penalty (4 to 12 seconds after placing the ball) takes a psychological toll, and increases the chance of missing. The most successful penalties are taken within 3 seconds.

9. DISGUISE YOUR BODY SHAPE

The pattern of your body as it takes the penalty is a dead giveaway to the keeper as to what you intend to do. Raising a balancing left arm before kicking with the right leg indicates that the ball will go right, and vice versa. At the very least, be aware of what your body's telling the keeper when you take the penalty.

10. PRACTICE MAKES PERFECT

Some people believe that you can practise all you like, but it won't make any difference as to how well you'll perform in a penalty shoot-out as the experience is so unique and intense. These people are wrong, and the stats back this up.

Put it this way: since losing on penalties to Czechoslovakia at the 1976 European Championships, the German national team have included a rigorous penalty-taking practice regime into their training. The English national squad don't practise penalties, preferring instead to turn up and wing it.

Which approach works best?

The final whistle

So there we have it. In the unlikely event you're ever picked to represent the English national team in a penalty shoot-out (and you might as well be the way things are going), you'll be fully clued up as to how to proceed. Don't forget your shin pads.

> **TIP:** Don't worry about who takes the first penalty. A study of 95 penalty shoot-outs in the German FA Cup between 1986 and 2006 found 'no grain of truth' in the idea that taking the first kick in a shoot-out held any advantage whatsoever.

TOP 3
ENGLAND
PENALTY
MISSES
OF THE LAST
25 YEARS

Stuart Pearce

ENGLAND VS. WEST GERMANY

1990 WORLD CUP

Ingrained in the national psyche for oh-so many reasons, this semi-final match is still best remembered for two things: Paul 'Gazza' Gascoigne melting the hearts of the nation for the first and last time as he blubbed

uncontrollably at the realisation that his yellow card meant that he wouldn't be able to play if England made it to the final; and Stuart Pearce's missed penalty, which effectively meant that we'd lost and West Germany had won. Gazza's weren't the only tears that day.

Of course, Pearce's botched penalty wasn't technically the one that lost England the match, as Chris Waddle was the next England player to approach the spot, and put it over the cross bar. But Pearce's miss was the one that fatally dented morale, and is the one everyone remembers.

Imagine how different the 1990s might have been if this goal had gone in and we'd gone on to win the competition. The whole social fabric of the UK would have been different. There'd have been no Blur and Oasis, no 'Football's Coming Home', no Damien Hirst and no Tony Blair (possibly). Well done, Stuart Pearce. Cheers.

David Beckham
ENGLAND VS. PORTUGAL
EURO 2004

Incredible at the time, Beckham's unbelievably off-target 2004 penalty is jaw-dropping even now (go and look on YouTube if you don't

believe me). There's a palpable hush in the stadium as 'Becks' takes the first penalty, and even now you can sense real fear and respect from the Portuguese crowd, a sense of reverential awe as the world's most famous footballer approaches the spot of destiny. Then what does Goldenballs do? Skies it so far over the goal that it's in danger of hitting the Goodyear Blimp. Even now, years later, it's still baffling. How did he manage to cock it up so badly? (Beckham's haircut of that month – a close-cropped skinhead job designed to make him look serious and warrior-like – only added to his humiliation, making him look like a giant grumpy toddler who's dropped his ice cream.) The penalty itself was such an affront to logic – to what everyone expected to happen next – that even the Portuguese supporters looked confused, as if it might all be a *Beadle's About*-style practical joke.

This mammoth miss prompted a real joke – the cruel but fair 'You'll never guess what I found in my back garden the other day – the ball from Beckham's penalty! Ha ha ha!!!!' – which brightened the national mood a tiny fraction when every joker in the UK was telling it the next day. Just before the realisation sank in that we'd failed dismally, yet again, at the game we gave to the world.

To be fair, Beckham's foot slipped when he took this penalty – if you look again at the footage, he immediately turns round and despairingly gestures towards the treacherous turf where he planted his non-kicking foot. Depending on your point of view this either exonerates him or compounds his error by making it look as if he's blaming the pitch.

Gareth Southgate
ENGLAND VS. GERMANY
EURO 1996

Not a spectacular missed penalty – in fact, rather run-of-the-mill – but the stakes were arguably higher for this shoot-out than ever before. The England squad, six years after the heroic failure of Italia 1990, and their failure to qualify for the 1994 World Cup, had once more reached the semi-finals of a major competition. And remember, this was the mid-90s – football was bigger than ever before, and seemed to be intrinsically linked to the national mood, so a significant chunk of English pride was riding on this one. The fact that it was against traditional rivals Germany, on the hallowed home turf of Wembley, just made it all the more significant. Here was a chance for revenge.

   Tension mounted as each side scored a goal apiece, but neither were able to secure a victory. The game went to extra time, during which the deadlock continued. And so, with cruel irony, it went to penalties. Hearts were in mouths all over England as each penalty was taken, particularly when Stuart Pearce approached the spot (Pearce had of course managed to erase the shame of 1990, with his successful strike in the shoot-out against Spain in the previous round – the one where he rushed over to the Wembley corner flag and bellowed at the crowd. But this was Germany, and bad memories of 'that night' in Italy were strongly present. Pearce scored, however, and for a few futile minutes, the watching nation believed things might go England's way.)

   But in the end it didn't matter – after five penalties each the scores were tied, and up strode Gareth Southgate. His penalty was saved, and, with a sense of dreary inevitability, England were out. While it was almost worth it to see the looks on David Baddiel's and Frank Skinner's faces, it was a flinty heart indeed that didn't feel Southgate's pain as he trudged away from the goalmouth, carrying a nation's disappointment on his shoulders.

THE HISTORY

Given how much misery the penalty has caused the English nation, it will come as no surprise to learn that an Englishman didn't invent it. That dubious honour is credited to William 'Master Willie' McCrum from Milford, County Armagh, Northern Ireland, a businessman and amateur goalkeeper who came up with the idea way back in 1890.

OF THE PENALTY

McCrum was a terrible businessman, and an even worse gambler, but he was a very keen goalkeeper and a huge fan of football in general, and played in goal for his local team in Milford. Football and the rules of the game itself were a bit more 'fluid' back then, and physical assaults, fights and casual violence were very much part of the game.

Many local matches would dissolve into out-and-out rucking, and post-match charges of manslaughter were not unusual.

It was from his lonely position in the Milford goalmouth that McCrum had his brainwave. Why not bring in a 'penalty' system to rein in on-pitch violence? And, if so, what better penalty than a deliberately staged shot on the offending team's goal?

McCrum's great-grandson, literary critic Robert McCrum, insists that only a goalkeeper could have come up with an idea as tragic and heroic as this, and he may well be onto something. The goalkeeper is the focus of attention in a penalty kick; he's a second away from either being the man who lost it all or the man of the match. It certainly fits well with what we know of Master Willie's melodramatic temperament. Either way, the idea was formally proposed to the Irish Football Association, who in turn presented it to the International Football Association Board.

Who hated it.

It's interesting for the modern reader to hear the main reason they considered it a bad idea. Accepting the idea of penalties for 'ungentlemanly conduct' would force the sportsmen of the day to admit that 'ungentlemanly conduct' did actually occur on the pitch, something that most were loath to admit. Robert McCrum dug up the following quote from the legendary (and slightly bonkers) C B Fry, detailing his objections. Fry held that the very notion of the penalty was: 'a standing insult to sportsmen . . . a rule which assumes that players intend to trip, hack and push opponents and to behave like cads of the most unscrupulous kidney.'

Finally, after a great deal of debate, the board approved the idea on 2 June 1891, and the rule was introduced in the 1891–92 season. The world's first penalty kick in a professional football match was given to Wolverhampton Wanderers in their match against Accrington Stanley at Molineux, on 14 September 1891. A man called John Heath took the penalty, and managed to score, with Wolves going on to win with a 5–0 whitewash.

William McCrum himself didn't fare quite so well. In 1931, his debts forced him to sell the family cotton mill in Milford, and in 1932 he died – a lonely alcoholic in an Armagh boarding house.

How to Sketch Someone's Portrait

In an era in which men seem to be capable of less and less, it's good to remind ourselves of what a fully skilled Everybloke might be able to do. History is enriched by the presence of men of exceptional and wide-ranging ability, but in order to find a true Renaissance Man, we have to look at ... the Renaissance.

The archetypal Renaissance Man is of course Leonardo da Vinci. Painter, anatomist, musician, scientist, da Vinci mastered and surpassed all the key disciplines of his age. And he designed a tank. And a helicopter.

But above all, he was an artist, and artistic endeavour was the cornerstone of his achievements. Leonardo painted some of the most iconic images of all time, and, legend has it, could write with one hand while sketching with the other.

Could we revive the idea of the Renaissance Man? At the very least, could we add sketching and drawing to our armoury of easily rediscovered man skills?

There was only one way to find out.

The aim

In at the deep end as ever, our aim here is to improve your drawing skills to a point where you can offer your services as a professional street artist. To do this, you must get your portrait-drawing skills up to scratch, from 'is that supposed to be a dog or what?' to 'marketable'.

Basics

There are many types of sketch, ranging from the ones you do on a napkin in a balti house at the end of a drunken night to explain the offside rule, all the way to the sketchbooks of Leonardo and Michelangelo themselves – which, though rough, are works of art in their own right, especially in their depictions of the human form.

If there's one thing that scrutinising the notebooks of the masters teaches us, it's that a successful sketch doesn't merely render the person or object as seen – it captures something of their essential nature.

This makes our job much harder. As we're going to be sketching a portrait – a rough illustration of another person – it has to not only be technically competent, it must also strive to capture something of the essence of that person – i.e., actually look like that person to people who know them.

Why sketch?

If you're thinking, 'Pish! I have a perfectly good camera which can capture the many nuances of the human face far better than mere hand or eye,' then you've missed the point. Sketching is worth learning as it helps you to organise your thoughts and understand matters of structure, composition and perspective. It will enable you to better comprehend the overall shapes and the finer details of the world around you. It's also a great way to relax and, if you can do it well, it looks damned impressive.

As we shall discover.

JAMES MAY

You Will Need

• Pencils (of all different types of hardness) • Decent quality sketching paper • An eraser

---

Later on, of course, you can sketch in charcoal or pastel or ink or anything you like, but for our purposes, pencil will suffice.

Before you start

Before you start for real – DON'T read any of the instructions just yet. The first thing you should do is go ahead and just draw a face without reading any of the lessons listed below. Don't deliberately do it badly – try and sketch the best portrait of someone you possibly can. Keep this drawing to one side, and we'll compare it with your later work in a bit. When your 'later work' actually exists.

After you've done that, you can now learn to draw a face properly.

Drawing a human face: Step-by-step

STEP 1: Place the features

- People's heads are basically an 'irregular ellipse' – an inverted egg shape to you and me – with the narrow part at the bottom. Draw this first.

- Excellent. Now draw a vertical line through the middle, to orient the bilateral symmetry of the face. Human faces obey an imperfect symmetry around this line. (You can skip this part if you're Picasso anytime after 1907 or so.)

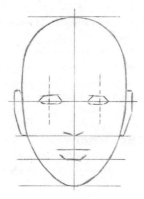

- Just below halfway down your face, draw a horizontal line. This is your eye line. Children usually draw eyes way up at the top of the head, but if you look in a mirror with your face held level, you'll see they're usually located on this line.

- Halfway between that line and the bottom of the egg shape (the base of the chin), draw another line. That's your nose line. Then, halfway between that line and the chin, draw another small line. This is your mouth line. Human beings come in all shapes and sizes, so this is only a rough guide to the location of features on the face, but it's broadly correct. You can fine-tune it to an individual's physiognomy later.

- The first line you drew – the eye line – is about the length of four eyes, and the eyes themselves are situated roughly half an eye in from each side (or half an eye from the central vertical line). Like so:

- So you've fixed your eyes. Now draw the nose, with the bottom of the nose resting on the nose line and working upwards.

- Then draw your mouth, balancing it on the mouth line and working up.

- Then add ears and hair. Ears start at just above the eye line. You should start drawing the hair from the parting outwards. Look for the general shape of the hair and focus on that rather than individual strands.

Ta-dah!

The point of this exercise is to get you comfortable with drawing the face, and situating the features on it.

JAMES MAY

Please note that this is the work of a professional illustrator, and not from the pencil of James May.

STEP 2: Draw the head from all angles

The above would be all you needed if human beings only ever came at you head on. Sadly, most of them don't, so you need to practise drawing the head, with the features correctly placed on it, from all angles.

Fortunately, the ratios we learned above remain constant wherever the head is positioned, so start by drawing the basic egg-shaped face from above and below (a and b).

An egg from the side is still egg-shaped, however, and so for drawing the face side-on you have to draw the head as a sphere on top of a smaller block (c), then locate the features in the same way you've done previously (d).

Use the block-and-sphere method whenever you draw the face side-on.

> **TIP:** One of the most useful facial positions to learn is the three-quarter face, used in many classic portraits. Make sure you can place the features correctly in a three-quarter profile.

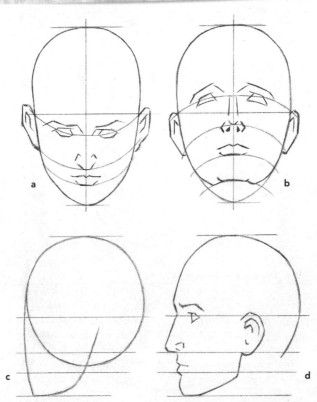

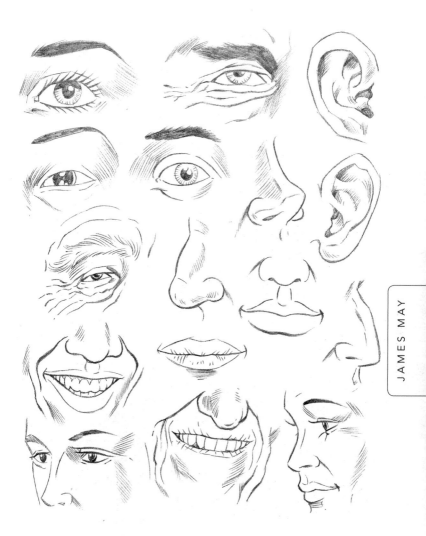

STEP 3: Learn to draw individual features

Eyes, ears, hair, noses – anything to do with the human face varies
hugely from person to person. As we're seeking to draw an accurate
likeness of an individual from life, it's in our interests to get good at
drawing anything that might be put in front of us. Practise drawing
individual features as much as you can, then try drawing them together.
It's also going to come in mighty useful if you can draw beards,
moustaches, spectacles, etc.

Once again, these are the work of a professional illustrator and not the work of James May.

STEP 4: Drawing expressions

So far, all our drawings have been of expressionless androids, which is great for drawing most politicians but not much use for normal human beings. Get used to drawing expressive features – happy, sad, cunning, gleeful, warm, bored, scared – and get used to capturing how the face looks when emotions course through it.

> **TIP:** Don't be afraid to copy from photos, comics or other illustrations, just so you understand how different expressions work, and what they do to the features.

STEP 5: Light and shade

You won't need to know everything about the delicate interplay of light and shade, but you'll need to know the rudiments. Make sure you understand how light hits an object, how to render this successfully in pencil, and how to apply those rules to the human face, and your portrait.

> **TIP:** Though you don't need to know that much anatomy, it helps if you're at least aware of the basics. Make sure you know where the various muscles of the face are, and what they do.

> **TIP:** Practise by sketching different objects – an apple, a beer can, a Toblerone – with different light sources hitting them. (Ideally, you should have a bust of the human face that you can draw in different lights, but this may not be possible if you don't actually live in a museum.)

STEP 6: Take it to the street

If you're going to draw people from life, the best way to do it is to get out there and actually do so. No matter how much you practise all of the above at home, your skills will only ever be academic unless you can successfully draw people from life.

> **TIP:** The big one – practice. Practise as much as you can, and keep your drawings. If you do even just half an hour a day, you'll be amazed how quickly you improve, week by week.

> **TIP:** If you're really serious about learning all this stuff, you're best off enrolling in a life-drawing class. It's interesting, immediate and fun and you will get to see at least one person in the nuddy.

Now compare the drawing you made following these instructions to the one you did earlier. You should notice a marked (and therefore encouraging and inspiring) improvement in your drawing skills.

You can draw! Now go and design a helicopter.

SOME FURTHER TIPS:

- Don't fuss over accuracy at this stage. Sketching is about getting the general impression of your subject on paper first and foremost. Learn to ignore the details and focus on the actual 'bigger picture' – get acquainted with what you absolutely need to put on the paper and what you can leave out.

- If you're sketching people outdoors, learn to work fast. Speed is of the essence, as your unpaid models will move around quite a lot.

- If you're serious about drawing and want to learn more, there are plenty of good books on it, many of which will include tutorials on stuff we didn't have time to go into here – perspective, composition, proportion, etc.

- Find the grade of pencil (or charcoal, or pen, or whatever) that you feel most comfortable with. Do a few warm-up exercises before you start, just to get comfortable. Drawing circles, spirals and cubes help with precision, and continuous line drawings (where you don't take your pencil from the page) help to loosen up your drawing muscles.

- Don't expect every drawing to be a masterpiece, but do remember to keep the best ones.

Here are some of my efforts...

Regrettably, this is the work of James May and his pencil.

So is this. Dan the soundman's eyes are not really this close together.

Many
AD 20/11

This one is a Roman centurion.

The one at top right is actually a woman.

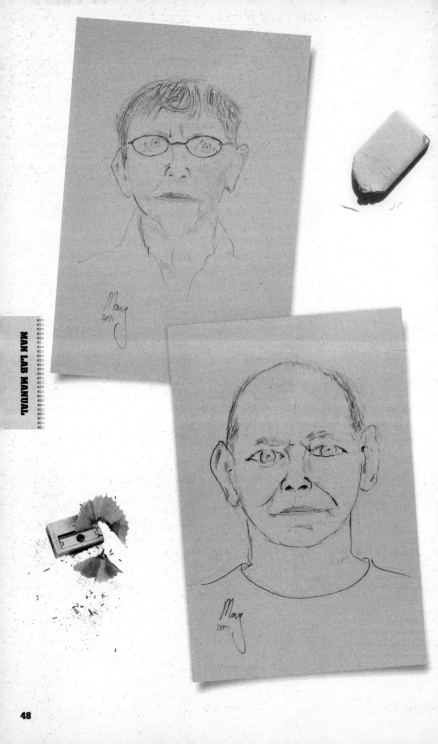

More dazzling masterpieces from the unresting HB of James May.

Fixing a Toaster

Toasters probably go wrong more than any other household appliance, especially if you buy a cheap one. To be fair, they're built with this in mind – a toaster isn't really something that gets handed down through the family.

Nonetheless, it's expensive and annoying to keep on buying new toasters every year and so, with that in mind, here are some handy tips on repair and maintenance that might lengthen the lifespan of what is undoubtedly your most-used cooking appliance.

Know your toaster

A toaster is basically made up of four things – a heating element, a timer, a carriage and a latch. A heating element toasts the toast, a timer times how long the bread stays in, the carriage is the wire frame inside that holds the bread, and the latch is the clip at the bottom of the toaster to hold things in place while they're being toasted.

With all this in mind, let's fix a toaster.

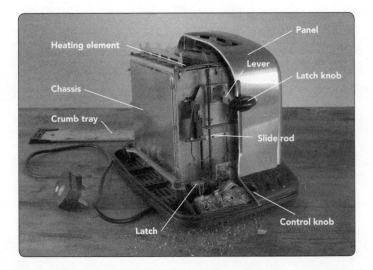

Panel
Heating element
Lever
Latch knob
Chassis
Crumb tray
Slide rod
Control knob
Latch

! *Don't meddle with a toaster that's under warranty – such meddling would invalidate it. Or with one that's still plugged in.*

Fixing the latch

One of the most common toaster ailments is also one of the easiest to fix –
namely, the annoying situation when the carriage no longer stays down.

Unplug the toaster. Unscrew and open the service panel on the toaster
(either on the side, or on the base) and undo any other fixtures or fittings
such as the latch knob (the thing you use to move the carriage down and
lock it) that might prevent you removing the panel completely.

Once you can see the latch, and where it connects and locks to keep
the carriage in place, you can usually see what the problem is. Very often
it's a build-up of crumbs, or other food-based blockage. Carefully remove
the blockage (you can use a can of compressed air for this, or even a small
screwdriver if it's exceptionally stubborn, but take care not to damage the
other components).

If the latch is bent out of shape, use needlenose pliers to reshape it.
While you're there you might also want to lubricate the carriage rod, on
which the whole assembly travels, but remember to use a lubricant that
has a high tolerance for heat and won't catch fire. You won't get your Man
Lab Toaster Repair Badge if your house burns down.

Re-assemble the toaster, and replace the service panel. Test it (see
overleaf).

> **TIP:** A lot of toaster malfunctions are caused by nothing more complicated
> than toast crumbs building up inside and damaging the mechanism. To prevent
> this, empty the crumb tray more often than 'never', which is probably how
> often you currently do it.

> **TIP:** Sticking your fingers, or a buttery knife, into a toaster to pull bread out
> is stupid for oh-so-many reasons – mostly to do with heat and mains electricity.
> We've all done it without thinking, but that doesn't make it right. Get some
> small wooden tongs and use those. You can even buy them with a magnet
> attached so they'll stick to the side of your toaster.

Recalibrating your toaster's thermostat

Another common toaster ailment is when the thermostat goes, leaving
you with a toaster that doesn't toast (or toasts too much). In order to
remedy this, you'll have to re-set the thermostat.

Take the service panel off, as described above. As well as the toaster's
workings, you will see some basic controls. One of these will be the thermostat
– a simple device that regulates temperature. It will have a calibration knob, or
possibly a screw. Turn this to adjust the thermostat settings.

Fixing the latch

Obviously there are no hard and fast rules here, but usually turning the knob away from the solenoid switch lengthens the toasting time, and turning towards it will shorten it.

Rebuild your toaster and try it out. This should have fixed the problem, but if it hasn't worked you can either try again or admit defeat and accept that your toaster is indeed 'brown bread'.

Legal notice: Always unplug the toaster before any repairs and – even more obviously – wait till the toaster's cool before you start probing around in it. Electricity is dangerous. Don't use your toaster in the bath, etc., etc.

> **TIP:** Refer to the toaster's manual. This should tell you exactly where things like the thermostat are. If you haven't kept the manual, a lot of companies now simply put them online, so check on the interweb.

> **TIP:** If it takes you more than an afternoon to fix the toaster, you might want to give in and buy a new one. Don't attempt to repair anything more complicated than a bog-standard toaster – such as a programmable electronic toaster, for instance – as you do not have a degree in electronic engineering, and you will break it. Even though it's already broken.

MAN LAB MANUAL

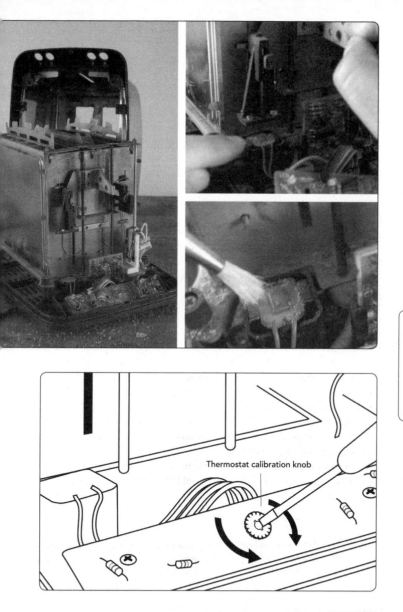

Thermostat calibration knob

TIP: If the element – possibly the most crucial part of your toaster – has gone, it's beyond repair and you can save time by simply junking it and buying another. Your toaster is indeed toast and not toasting at all.

tool of the week: the chisel

Ah, the humble chisel. To serious woodworkers, it's the pride of their armoury, the very definition of a 'tool of the trade'. Yet to the uninitiated, it's the ultimate bodger's friend, a blunt instrument used to whack, bludgeon, score, scratch, pry open, or – in extreme cases – even used to stir paint. We say: enough of this nonsense. Chisels are your friends, and it's high time you learned to use them properly.

Yes, you.

Chisel basics

The chisel is an ancient tool – they were widely used in ancient Egypt, but had been around for a long time even then. Ancient Egyptian chisels are instantly recognisable to the modern eye as chisels, as the basic design hasn't really changed a bit. They consist of a sharp end you put to the wood (or stone) and a blunt end that you thwack with a hammer.

But there's a lot more to them than that. Although a chisel may look simple, and its purpose obvious, using one properly requires skill and co-ordination.

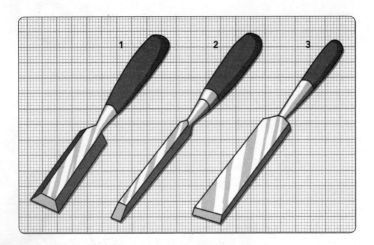

Chisels you need

There are a great many different types of chisel available, but, for basic home DIY, there are really only three types you'll need. They are:

1. Bevel-edged chisels: These are the classic woodworking chisels – thin-bladed chisels used for finessing and fine slicing jobs, such as 'chamfering' an edge or paring wood down in shaving strokes. The thinly-bevelled edge helps to achieve this and also makes it easier to access corners and hard-to reach places. The bevel-edged chisel is also designed to be guided by the thumb – using the right hand (say) on the handle, the left thumb is placed on the bevel to guide the chisel, giving a slicing motion onto the wood.

2. Mortise chisels: Stouter and heavier chisels, with a square edge, used for cutting grooves and deep mortises into wood. These chisels have long, thick blades, and both blade and handle are usually designed to take a lot of punishment. The sturdy blade also allows wood to be levered out of a mortise.

> **TIP:** It's a good idea to buy a few mid-price chisels, just so you can use them for all the borderline bodging jobs we mentioned earlier (apart from stirring paint, which I will not condone). It's not worth using an expensive, well-sharpened chisel to scrape excess glue from wood, but you still need to get the glue off; so keep some bog-standard chisels in reserve and the good, sharp ones for when you really need them.

3. Firmer chisels: A sort of mix between the two, this is your all-purpose chisel, with a variety of basic uses. This chisel is best used for roughing out your work in wood, and you can then complete the finer work with a bevel-edged chisel. As a general rule, bevel-edged chisels are used purely by hand, firmer chisels are struck with a mallet. (All the above are for wood only. For masonry work and wrecking, you'll need cold chisels and bolsters. We haven't the time to go into them here, but suffice to say they're basically big metal chisels you hit with a lump hammer.)

Sharpen up

Never has the old adage 'You're more likely to cut yourself with a blunt tool than a sharp one' been more true than when applied to the chisel (see also 'Chisel safety', p.61). A blunt chisel will cut unevenly, and catch in the wood, causing you to hit your fingers with the hammer, and swear loudly (at the very least). So make sure it's nice and sharp before you begin. Sharpen it on a special chisel-sharpening stone – you can buy these from any good DIY shop.

Crucial to chisel sharpness is a flat back, so make sure that you polish the back of the blade to a precise flatness. After all, the back of the chisel is also part of the cutting edge – professionals spend time on this before they even use a new chisel, and will then polish the flat side regularly, a habit that's worth taking up. After sharpening the beveled edge, the back will have developed a slight burr. This needs removing.

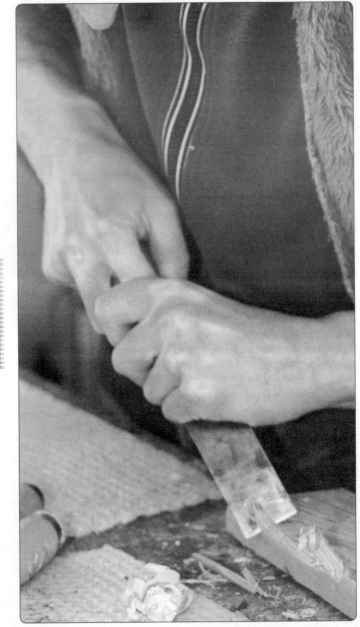

Using the chisel

Like everything worth doing, mastering a chisel takes time, so don't attempt anything too complex straight off the bat. Even when you finally do need to use a chisel, make sure that as much excess wood as possible has been removed, using a saw or a drill, as this will make your job much easier. Patience is key: chisels don't respond well to being hurried, and an ill-timed strike or cut can ruin hours of hard work. Don't be tempted to make large cuts, as this greatly increases the possibility of both mistakes and accidents. Guide the chisel with one hand and carefully apply force – whether by pushing or hitting – with the other.

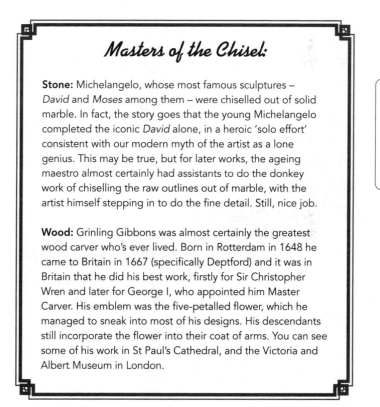

Masters of the Chisel:

Stone: Michelangelo, whose most famous sculptures – *David* and *Moses* among them – were chiselled out of solid marble. In fact, the story goes that the young Michelangelo completed the iconic *David* alone, in a heroic 'solo effort' consistent with our modern myth of the artist as a lone genius. This may be true, but for later works, the ageing maestro almost certainly had assistants to do the donkey work of chiselling the raw outlines out of marble, with the artist himself stepping in to do the fine detail. Still, nice job.

Wood: Grinling Gibbons was almost certainly the greatest wood carver who's ever lived. Born in Rotterdam in 1648 he came to Britain in 1667 (specifically Deptford) and it was in Britain that he did his best work, firstly for Sir Christopher Wren and later for George I, who appointed him Master Carver. His emblem was the five-petalled flower, which he managed to sneak into most of his designs. His descendants still incorporate the flower into their coat of arms. You can see some of his work in St Paul's Cathedral, and the Victoria and Albert Museum in London.

JAMES MAY

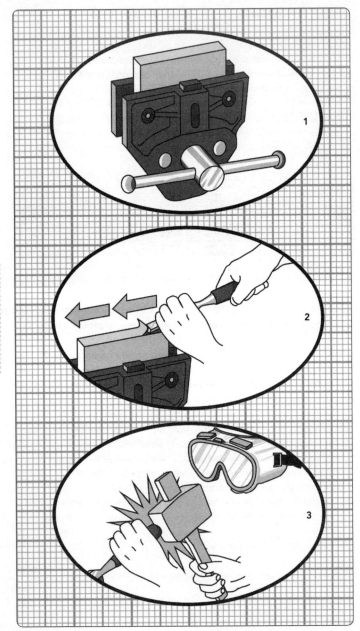

Top Jobs for Chisels

- Cutting out a neat recess for a hinge, strike plate, door lock, etc
- Cutting a dovetail joint (or pretty much any wood joint)
- 'Shaving' a wooden surface smooth, if you can't use a plane

Chisel safety

Never, ever misuse a chisel. When you consider that you're putting brute force behind an extremely sharp blade, you can see that the potential for hideous accidents is enormous. The chisel requires respect.

SOME BASIC RULES:

- Before you even start, always secure the piece of wood you're working on with a vice or clamp (1).
- Always cut away from yourself (2). Or, as somebody once put it, 'Always cut towards your friends.' (They were speaking metaphorically of course. Don't cut your friends.)
- Always keep your fingers behind the 'leading edge' of the chisel. Make this a habit from the start, as it will save you from injury if and when the chisel slips.
- Never allow the ghost of Jacques Cousteau anywhere near your favourite chisels (3).

JAMES MAY

SAVING MEN'S FASHION

LG

One of the great ironies of the male existence is that the last place a chap should turn to for advice is a 'men's lifestyle magazine'. In these, one will find absolutely no advice on how to remove a broken exhaust stud from a Honda 400/4 or how to play the mandolin, just hundreds of pages about clothes. And even here they tend to be contradictory. On the one hand they celebrate the sheer variety of clothing available for blokes – shirts, coats, terrible caps in 'distressed' (i.e. ruined) fabrics – and then on another spread they try to tell you that the male wardrobe can be pared down to just eight items.

I have more sympathy with the second notion, but eight still seems like an awfully big number. Wouldn't life be easier, and wouldn't a massive burden of trend-related tyranny be lifted from us, if there was a single, all-purpose piece of clothing that served every purpose, and looked equally at home in the garage or the cocktail lounge?

I set out to discover if such a miraculous item of clothing already existed and, if not, to make it.

Fashion – the essentials

In the past, I have been accused of possessing a slightly dubious fashion sense. Good. In our cities, there are no statues to blokes who famously looked a bit dapper. They are of men who conquered continents, discovered bacteria or saw off the Luftwaffe.

But the sad fact is that I'm on TV, and therefore a ponce, and I've amassed quite a lot of clothing over the years. But do I actually need it all? Come to that, do I actually need any of it? After a cursory look at my creaking wardrobe, I began to think that both the piece of furniture and those men's mags could be a lot slimmer.

As mentioned, one of these mags recently stated that the ideal male wardrobe can be reduced to a mere eight essentials – a suit, a white shirt, a tie, a pair of jeans, a V-neck sweater, a white T-shirt, smart shoes and casual shoes.

But I think there could be seven redundant things in that list.

The miracle garment

I am suggesting that a man's wardrobe can be pared right back to but one single item of clothing – a garment that would fulfil all of man's requirements, both sartorial and practical, and embody the best that man can aspire to.

But what would such an item of clothing look like? Well, let's consider all the requirements we have of this hypothetical *über*-garment.

- It should be practical and purposeful (so, lots of pockets).
- It should keep you warm, and dry (so, be made of thick material and not allow draughts).
- It should keep things like sawdust and chip fat away from your gentleman's area.
- It should double as acceptable wear for any social occasion (the Last Night of the Proms, the Ambassador's Reception, Glastonbury).

So, with those rules in place, we can now start to get a rough idea of what this miraculous item would look like.

Broadly speaking, it would be a one-piece coverall made of a tough (though flexible) material, allowing it to be worn during strenuous manual labour as well as being ideal for simply lounging around in; with breast and hip pockets, requiring only one zip or set of buttons to fasten.

Now we've described it, this garment sounds strangely familiar.

The boilersuit – menswear par excellence

The boilersuit was developed for use in the boiler rooms of the steam era (although the general concept is quite a bit older). The suit was designed so that a maintenance man could physically climb into the cooled-down firebox of a steam engine – the chamber where the coal is shovelled in – and repair or clean it. Thanks to the unique design of the boilersuit, the maintenance man could do all the repairing and cleaning he liked without worrying about his clothing getting snagged or caught, or the boiler accidentally delivering a hefty payload of soot or coal dust down his trousers. These practical benefits of the boilersuit ensured that it caught on, and by the 1920s its use had spread into many different kinds of industry.

The boilersuit has changed little since then, becoming something of a design classic. And why should it need to change? To put it in the language of the fashionista, the boilersuit is a timeless piece invoking the spirit of the working man and the honest toil of the Industrial Age.

Imagine if we all wore boilersuits. Men would be liberated from fashion fascism to stride the earth in a practical, sensible manner. There'd be no need for magazines like GQ or fashion pundits like Gok Wan or Laurence Llewellyn-Bowen.

All of this was more than enough to convince me that the boilersuit was long overdue a comeback. My mission, therefore, was to restore this classic male outfit to its rightful place as a man's clothing of choice.

Churchill and the boilersuit

Before we go any further, it's worth mentioning that I'm certainly not history's first champion of the boilersuit. No less a person than Winston Leonard Spencer Churchill – a man who you'd think would run a mile from anything that would make him look even more like a gigantic baby than he did already – embraced this giant romper suit wholeheartedly.

During the Blitz, the boilersuit caught on among a British civilian population who now had to make a quick exit from places, often in the middle of the night. The suit proved itself to be the ultimate in air-raid chic as it could be donned in under a minute – very handy if you were called upon to leg it to an Anderson shelter at 4 am. The boilersuit even acquired a new nickname – the Siren Suit.

The Siren Suit's popularity in a Britain threatened by the Nazi menace was given the official seal of approval by Winston, who took to wearing his own suits at all hours of the day and night. Let us not forget that fact: the very embodiment of British defiance during World War II fought off the Axis powers while wearing a boilersuit.

Being Churchill, however, he didn't wear just any old boilersuit. Winnie designed his own, and had different ones made up for different activities and occasions. There were boilersuits made of red, green and blue velvet, which Churchill would wear at home (with specially-made monogrammed slippers). There was a blue serge one, which he actually wore to sit for a portrait. There was another made of pinstriped grey wool, with an extra-large waistline to accommodate his ample girth. Thankfully, many of these important and iconic items of men's fashion have not been lost – the green velvet suit is currently on display at Chartwell, Churchill's home in Kent, and the pinstriped number was sold at Sotheby's in 2002. Reportedly, it hadn't been washed since Churchill last wore it, and still smelled of victory.

Although a wholehearted supporter of the boilersuit, Churchill did encounter one of the signature problems men have faced with this garment, namely a painful and hasty zipping up after going for a wee. Edmund Murray, one of Churchill's bodyguards, recalls Churchill roaring in pain when he was having trouble with his zip.

With such a memorable and patriotic endorsement, you'd think that the boilersuit's future was assured. But, sadly, victory saw the end of the suit as political weapon. Without the clout of a serving prime minister behind it, the boilersuit went into a vertiginous decline.

A decline I shall set about reversing.

Boilersuit chic – on the streets

In order to gauge the reaction of the ironic, postmodern, jaded populace of our day to the boilersuit, I decided, rather bravely, to wear one to a fashion event. Thus it was that I attended Student Fashion Week, at Earls Court, dressed in my own one-piece.

In undertaking this valuable and important experiment, I learned the following things:

- Wearing a boilersuit to a fashion event is generally assumed by most observers to be nothing more than a joke.
- It also means you are likely to be taken for the man who's come to fix the bogs rather than an ambassador for cutting-edge style.
- You might not be able to get in to this or any other posh venue at all, owing to an arcane and unfathomable set of rules known as a 'dress code', which places the boilersuit beneath even 'casual'.

Slightly chastened, I repaired to the Man Lab to rethink my assault on the world of men's fashion. I realised we might need to make some slight concessions to prevailing notions of 'style' if this was going to catch on. What the boilersuit needed was an upgrade.

The boilersuit – a bit half-baked

Now although the boilersuit is eminently practical, I would be the first to say that they aren't what you'd call 'flattering'. Take a man with the chiselled, perfect physique of Michelangelo's *David*, say, stick him in a boilersuit, and he'll end up the same shape in outline as any other man in a boilersuit, i.e., the shape of an unemployed Teletubby who's been made to give back the antenna headgear.

A particular problem is the rump of the boilersuit, which tends to sag catastrophically, making the unfortunate wearer look like someone who's had a rather large accident in his trousers. The belly can also sag in a similar way. Also – if you want to get technical – the boilersuit denies the limbs any contour or definition, so that they look like they've been rolled out of Plasticine.

The answer was simple. We needed to make the boilersuit 'tailored' and then, with a few simple amendments, it could be made to fit every likely occasion – 'smart', 'party', 'office' and 'workshop'.

The boilersuit – re-imagined

I set up a sewing machine, intent on implementing the alterations that would transform the boilersuit from a piece of light-industrial wear to a fashion statement that would stun to silence the catwalks of Paris and

Milan, and re-invent male identity for the twenty-first century.

Five minutes later, I remembered that I didn't know how to operate a sewing machine. But what I did manage to do was draft the following rough plan, in the spirit of Churchill, showing how the boilersuit might – with just a few subtle alterations – be improved.

Here [opposite], then, is our redesigned boilersuit. An industrial suit for the post-industrial age.

There are plenty of other additions you can make to your boilersuit, but remember – any specific alterations you make will detract from your boilersuit's universality and go-anywhere practical convenience. If you have your name sewn in gold lettering across the shoulders of your suit, it will be less appropriate for a funeral. If you decide to make your suit as formal as possible, wearing it on a construction site to do manual labour will make you look like some sort of bad performance artist. Remember the example set by Churchill – your suit must be genuinely all-purpose.

Boilersuits – a new dawn

Thus it was that we transformed the world of men's fashion, reduced the male wardrobe to its bare essentials, returned the boilersuit to its rightful place at the vanguard of contemporary *haute couture* and paid tribute to the memory of Winston Churchill.

A good day's work.

Boilersuit Variations

Water resistant – for plumbers.

Fire retardant – for firemen and electricians.

Quilted – padded all over with an extra-thick layer for warmth, handy for exterior work in the cold.

Ladies' – amazingly for a garment that's essentially shapeless and unisex, there are female versions available, with a larger chest area and pleats.

Orange – standard issue prison wear in US jails/death row of US jails/Guantanamo Bay. Now also a standard fancy-dress costume for Halloween, and terrible stag nights.

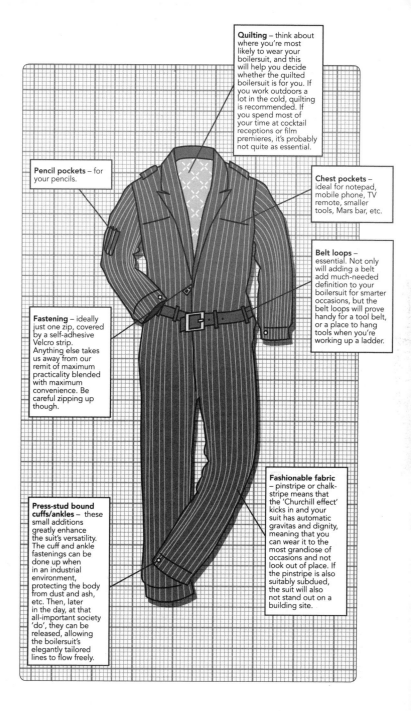

Quilting – think about where you're most likely to wear your boilersuit, and this will help you decide whether the quilted boilersuit is for you. If you work outdoors a lot in the cold, quilting is recommended. If you spend most of your time at cocktail receptions or film premieres, it's probably not quite as essential.

Pencil pockets – for your pencils.

Chest pockets – ideal for notepad, mobile phone, TV remote, smaller tools, Mars bar, etc.

Belt loops – essential. Not only will adding a belt add much-needed definition to your boilersuit for smarter occasions, but the belt loops will prove handy for a tool belt, or a place to hang tools when you're working up a ladder.

Fastening – ideally just one zip, covered by a self-adhesive Velcro strip. Anything else takes us away from our remit of maximum practicality blended with maximum convenience. Be careful zipping up though.

Press-stud bound cuffs/ankles – these small additions greatly enhance the suit's versatility. The cuff and ankle fastenings can be done up when in an industrial environment, protecting the body from dust and ash, etc. Then, later in the day, at that all-important society 'do', they can be released, allowing the boilersuit's elegantly tailored lines to flow freely.

Fashionable fabric – pinstripe or chalk-stripe means that the 'Churchill effect' kicks in and your suit has automatic gravitas and dignity, meaning that you can wear it to the most grandiose of occasions and not look out of place. If the pinstripe is also suitably subdued, the suit will also not stand out on a building site.

Fixing a Clock

'Time may change me, but I can't trace time!' So sang David Bowie in 1972, which could be Dave's way of saying his clock's broken (but is probably a metaphor or something). However, if you, like Mr Bowie, find yourself suffering from the misery of a broken or faulty clock, here are some proper old-school tips on repairing it.

Clock repair – a boring disclaimer

The repair of most complicated and/or antique timepieces is a precise art best left to the professionals, or people who've at least taken some kind of clock-mending course and have the first clue about how a clock works.

Clock repair – becoming more interesting

But that said, there are some quick and easy fixes which might save you having to take a clock to be mended.

Here they are:

Clock is moving too fast/slow

Probably the most common clock-related problem. With most modern battery-operated clocks, you just need to reset the hands with a dial at the back, but with an older clock it can be a bit trickier.

If your clock is a pendulum clock, then fixing this is easy. If the clock is running slowly, simply raise the nut below the pendulum a little. This will cause the pendulum to swing faster, thus speeding up the clock. The opposite trick of lowering the nut and slowing the pendulum 'bob' will slow down a clock that's running too fast. If the clock consistently runs too fast, it may be fitted with the wrong bob. A professional clock mender will be able to diagnose this, and should have spares.

Pendulum clocks will also lose time, or indeed stop completely, if the clock is on an uneven surface, causing uneven swing. The best remedy for this is to lift one side of the clock up a small amount and listen to the tick. If it improves and becomes more even then put a coin or a piece of cardboard under that side. If it stops or gets worse, do the same with the other side.

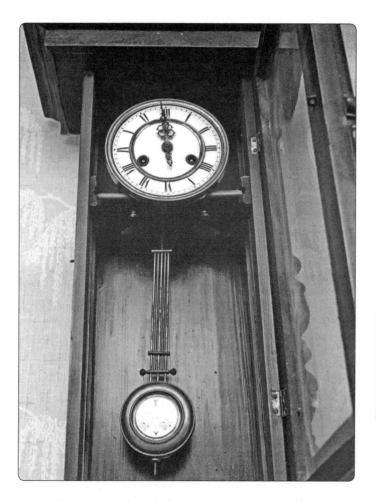

Some clockwork clocks have a hole in the face, usually just above the numeral '12', which allows access to a small shaft at the top of the movement, by which you can adjust the speed the clock runs at. Using a key, you can turn this mechanism slowly until the clock corrects itself (some clocks even have the letters S and F for Slow and Fast by the hole, so you can tell which way you're adjusting it). The key is very small – unless you have the original, get yourself a watch key of the right size.

TIP: Temperature and humidity affect the workings of clocks, as the workings can swell or contract, affecting accuracy. Make sure the clock isn't somewhere too cold, hot or damp.

Make any adjustments very slowly and gradually. Rapid adjustments can damage the clock workings. The original object of this S/F mechanism was to avoid having to turn a great big Victorian black marble clock around on the mantelpiece to get at the pendulum (however, this mechanism is only capable of turning two or three turns either way, and will only do fine adjustments of a couple of minutes or so at a time).

Clock stops entirely

With a pendulum clock, this may be due, once again, to the clock being situated on an uneven surface, resulting in the pendulum hitting the rear of the clock case. To fix this, simply move the clock.

In an electric clock, this could be due to a loose connection. Unplug the clock or take the battery out, unscrew the back and check all the connections. I wouldn't advise tinkering at an amateur level with any clock that runs off mains electricity, so don't.

In a clockwork clock, the problem might be as simple as dust or other detritus in the mechanism. Open the clock up and inspect the workings. Gently and carefully remove any fluff, lint, etc, from the cogs and springs (a cotton bud can be handy for this, but make sure it doesn't shed cotton wool in the mechanism). If any gears are worn out, you might have to get them replaced by a professional.

The workings of a stalled clockwork clock may simply need oiling. You can buy clock repair kits with all the necessary equipment for doing this, as well as a solution of ammonia for cleaning your clock's workings.

Loose hands

A common problem with cheap clocks. You know the kind of thing – you buy it, and a few months later, it's perpetually half-past-six as the clock hands sag under their own weight. In most cases this can be solved by stopping the clock and gently squeezing the base of the hands so that they grip the central shaft (stop sniggering).

This will only work if the hands are metal – if they're plastic, you might have to improvise, or simply give up and get another clock.

> **TIP:** Never turn the hands of a clock anti-clockwise. Some older clocks will be very easily damaged if this is done to them.

Clock is too noisy

There's not much you can do about this. Old-fashioned mechanical alarm clocks tend to be especially noisy; ironic, really, if you're trying to sleep. The solution is to move the clock to another room, but then of course it won't be available to wake you up. This is positively paradoxical.

> **TIP:** The mechanism of a clock is referred to as 'the movement'. Make it sound like you know what you're doing by calling it that at all times.

> **TIP:** If the clock stops entirely, it's always worth checking the hands too. They may be clashing. Carefully straighten them and set them going again.

Quick Tip

Making The Perfect Cup of Tea ✓

There are certain subjects that appear on the surface to be mundane and controversy-free, but turn out on closer examination to be among the most bitterly contested and controversial.

This small but select group of topics tends to be about the rules governing the minutiae of life, and how important it is to get them absolutely spot-on.

Perhaps the most important of these debates is the one about how to make the perfect cup of tea.

Thus it is in the interests of world peace, and furthering understanding between the nations of the Earth, that we humbly offer this guide to brewing up properly.

Trouble brewing

In one of his famous essays about the importance of the apparently trivial things that make life meaningful (see our section on building your own bar later in the book), George Orwell wrote at length about the importance of a correctly made cup of tea. He began by expressing surprise that no cookery book, to the best of his knowledge, contained a detailed, foolproof recipe for making a satisfying cup of tea, almost as if the average person were born with tea-making in their genes.

Orwell had no truck with this hit-and-miss approach, and devised no fewer than eleven Golden Rules for making the perfect cup of tea (see below). Some of these rules are simple common sense (use a teapot, use water that's absolutely at the boiling point, and so on) and other rules show their age a bit. Remember, when Orwell was writing, tea was still rationed and the tea bag was naught but a faraway dream.

Despite these flaws, Orwell's essay remained the standard work on the subject for a while, and the rules are worth repeating here.

George Orwell's rules for making perfect tea:

1. Use Indian or Ceylon tea, not Chinese. Orwell regarded Chinese tea as lacking in restorative qualities. 'One does not feel wiser, braver or more optimistic after drinking it.'

2. Tea should be made in small quantities, in a china or earthenware teapot, rather than in an urn.
3. Warm the pot on the hob beforehand.
4. Tea should be strong. Orwell noted that the older a person gets, the stronger they like their tea. He recommended six spoonfuls per quart.
5. Tea should be put straight into the pot, not strained (obviously, this was before the invention of the tea bag, a development I suspect Orwell would have hated).
6. The water should be poured into the teapot at the moment of boiling – bring the teapot to the kettle, not the other way around.
7. Stir the pot (Orwell even recommends shaking it), then let the leaves settle.
8. Tea should be taken from a 'cylindrical breakfast cup' (that's a 'mug' to you and me) rather than a shallow cup, which will make the tea go cold faster.

9. Pour the cream off the milk before using it. Cream gives tea a sickly taste.
10. Pour the tea into the cup first rather than the milk (but see below).
11. Tea should be taken without sugar. As far as Orwell was concerned, sugar destroyed the genuine tea taste, and should be avoided at all costs.

This was generally accepted as constituting a good rule-of-thumb guide until 2003, when the world of tea-making was rocked to its very foundations by new research from the Royal Society of Chemistry.

Royal brew
Dr Andrew Stapley, of Loughborough University's Chemical Engineering department, decided to put Orwell's rules to rigorous scientific testing, mixed of course with his own personal preferences. Here are the rules that Stapley disputed:

Rule 4: Orwell's tea is so strong it can stun a rhinoceros. Rather than six spoons per quart, try one per cup. Another old saw says 'one teaspoon per person and one for the pot'.

Rule 10: Both Orwell and Stapley, acting independently and decades apart, both identified this issue as the single most crucial and controversial of all. Namely: Should the milk or tea go in first? Stapley found that, scientifically speaking, Orwell was wrong. Adding the milk to the tea means that parts of the milk are, for a few crucial seconds, excessively heated. This over-heating causes the milk proteins to unfurl and clump together, like they do in UHT milk, and tea made in polystyrene cups (which tend to keep tea hot for too long). Obviously, this makes for a less-pleasant cuppa, so remember – milk goes in first.

Rule 11: (the one about 'no sugar') – untrue. Sugar actually complements the astringent taste of tea rather than dominating it, provided you don't put in too much.

Finally – The perfect cup of tea
It should be feasible, using the combined knowledge of both the literary titan and the chemical engineer from Loughborough, to devise the perfect formula for a cup of tea.

So: for our money, this is how a good cup of tea is made:

- Use Assam tea. Both Dr Stapley and Mr Orwell concurred that Indian tea is the best, though this was a personal preference in both cases.

- Use a clean, warm, china or earthenware teapot.
- Add 1 spoonful of tea (or one teabag) per cup.
- Use water that's absolutely at boiling point. Soft water is best.
- Stir the teapot.
- Leave to brew for three minutes.
- Once and for all: add the tea to the milk rather than the other way round.
- Add sugar if you like. Only use white sugar; don't add too much.
- Drink tea at 60–65°C. Any less will be too cold; any warmer and you'll slurp it, and shock the vicar with your base animal habits.
- Tea is best enjoyed in a tranquil, calm environment, and in a sitting position.

Sadly, we don't have time to address the age-old biscuit-dunking controversy. Maybe next time.

JAMES MAY

tool of the week: the drill

Drills. They've revolutionised home DIY in the last hundred or so years, by transforming themselves from hand-driven, turn-handle slog machines – in both senses, the very definition of the word 'boring' – to smart, sexy, easy-to-use essentials. Where would home DIY – or early 1980s horror films – be without this ultra-modern appliance?

Let's hear it for the drill.

Drill basics

The story of the drill begins with the bow drill, an extremely ancient device largely used to make fire, although it was also eventually applied to primitive woodwork (and, God help us, primitive dentistry). The Ancient Egyptians used the bow drill, as did the earlier Harappans in India. Thousands of years later, carpenter's braces and hand drills were invented, and eventually larger-scale pillar drills were devised that were powered by water and wind.

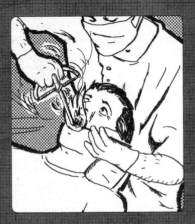

However, this story doesn't really get interesting until the invention of the electric drill in 1889, and the subsequent invention of the portable electric drill in 1895, which gave us the drill we're familiar with today – the sleek, portable, all-purpose tool, and staple of early 1980s 'video nasties'.

Drills you need

Two basic types:

Battery-powered cordless drill: An essential. If possible, get one with a spare battery so that at least one battery can charge up while you work. There are many good brands and names available and, as with all tools, it pays to spend a little bit extra. Lots of big DIY chains do their own cheap power drills, but they don't have much in the way of power, aren't built to last, and often have a very short battery life and no spare battery. Get a good one. You're making holes and it's important.

TIP: Never drill into masonry or brickwork with a lightweight cordless drill. It will damage the drill, possibly for good.

Cordless drills: Versatile and easy to use. Their cordless status makes them very convenient to use anywhere.

Hammer drill, or impact drill: The perfect companion to a cordless drill, a hammer drill has more welly and also utilises a hammering, thrusting action, giving the drill greater penetrating power. Until fairly recently, hammer drills needed to be plugged into the mains to gain the necessary extra power, but improvements in small motors and re-chargeable batteries mean there are now plenty of cordless hammer drills that can be used for drilling concrete and brickwork.

TIP: If you're planning on doing a lot of drilling into masonry, and brickwork, you'll need special equipment. Best to get a heavy-duty, mains-powered drill with a percussive action and a reverse gear. Phwoar.

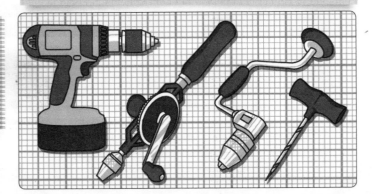

Hand drills

The secret of any good toolkit is that it should be well-stocked, thus offering the handyman a range of alternatives for solving a problem. This is especially relevant when we talk about drills. Electric drills are all very well, but they are massively over-used (and often badly used) and the results can be messy. Sometimes it pays to take things that little bit slower, which is why any good toolkit should also include the following old-fashioned manual drills.

A HAND DRILL

Due to the rise and rise of the electric drill, the traditional hand-wound drill, with its 'eggbeater' turning handle, has all but vanished from the casual workman's toolkit. This is a shame, as it is accurate, eminently controllable and satisfying to use. As you will find out by buying and using one.

A WOOD BRACE
This is a large crank handle, essentially for hand-turning the 'bit' into the wood. Unsurprisingly, they've been in use for hundreds of years and are reliable and simple tools. Proper carpenters will own more than a few of these, and you should have at least one.

A GIMLET
A very basic hand tool for drilling small holes. Handy to have as the slow hand-driven rotation means it's unlikely to split the wood. Very useful for making 'pilot holes' for bigger bits to follow.

> **TIP:** Carefully consider your drilling project, and don't be over-reliant on the electric drill. If a hand drill or brace will give a better, cleaner result, then use that instead.

Drill bits
There are many different types of drill bit, each designed for a specific task. Out of the hundreds of varieties of drill bit, the best known and most useful around the home or Man Lab are:

TWIST
Yer most common drill bit – a sturdy steel rod with a fluted cutting edge. The spiral cutting edge is actually an Archimedean screw, physics fans – meaning that it's effective at drawing the waste shavings out of the hole and away from the cutting point.

Twist bits are made either of high-speed steel (HSS) – which means they're suitable for wood, metal and plastic – or carbon steel, which means they're OK with wood and plastic, but too brittle to cope with drilling into metal.

Most electric drills come with a basic set of twist bits, including the vital pilot bit, used to drill holes in wood, into which screws can be driven.

One variation on the twist bit is the spur point bit, which has two raised spurs on the cutting edge, for increased accuracy while drilling into wood or plastic.

MASONRY
Usually used with a hammer drill, a masonry bit is a machine-milled bit with a very tough tungsten carbide insert at the drilling edge, for drilling into stone and brick.

AUGER

Auger bits are long, large, fluted bits designed for smooth boring and the effective removal of shavings of waste wood. They usually have a tip that resembles a screw shaft, for easier drilling, followed by the larger bore cutting edges, though some types have a single spur at the front for increased accuracy. They used to be compatible only with a hand-brace, but as most power drills now have multi-speed options, augers don't have to be used exclusively with hand drills any more, provided you go in on a slow setting.

SPADE (OR PADDLE)

Large, flat-headed bits for only the most imprecise wood drilling. They have two cutting edges, usually with spurs on them to clean the hole as they rotate. Only designed for use with power drills, this is one bit that is relatively easy to sharpen yourself.

COUNTERSINK BIT

Drill bit with a conical end, for making conical holes (see below).

Drill prep

Make sure you're using the right drill bit for the material you're about to drill into. Make sure the drill bit is securely fastened, either by twisting the chuck tight, or, in older or more heavy-duty models, tightening with a chuck key.

> TIP: Most chuck-key drills these days have the chuck key fixed to the power cord, for ease of use and so that you don't lose it. Nonetheless, it's best to keep a spare chuck key around just in case.

Using the drill

As ever, properly secure your work with clamps before you start, unless it's a wall, in which case it will be secure already.

Holding the drill so that the bit is at 90 degrees to the surface in both directions – both forward and back and side to side – proceed to slowly drill the hole. Allow the drill to find its own pace, and while some pushing is required, try not to force the drill as this will place stress on both the bit and the drill motor. Practise – make sure you become adept at drilling in, and then freeing the drill, without the bit sticking.

If you're assembling something out of wood, and want to conceal the screw heads, you'll need a countersink bit. This is a drill bit with a large conical head that will make a cone-shaped depression at the top of your pre-drilled screw hole. So, simply drill the hole first with a correctly sized pilot bit, then countersink the screw hole with a countersink bit so that when you drive the screw in, the head (which is basically shaped like an inverted cone) fills the countersink, and sits flush with the wood surface.

> **TIP:** Always have a good supply of spare drill bits – especially the smaller ones, which are liable to break, and which you will use a lot. Drill bits are very easy to lose or leave 'on site', so be careful to replace them in your kit as you go.

> **TIP:** Practise making holes, and then practise driving screws in and out of them until you get it right. Like knocking a nail in, it looks easy. Also like knocking a nail in, it often isn't.

> **TIP:** For increased accuracy, you might want to use a hammer and a centre punch to make a mark in the surface first, to stop the drill 'wandering'.

Top Jobs for Drills

- Drilling wood, metal, masonry
- Driving screws in (and driving them out)
- Countersinking the surface so that the screw heads sit neatly in their own recess

Drill safety

Make sure if you drill into a wall that you're not drilling into any water, gas or electricity mains (see the section on 'hammers' for more about this).

Make sure your posture is good (for the sake of the quality of the work, as well as your health). Wear goggles where necessary to protect your eyes and ear defenders, especially when drilling masonry.

What else didn't the Ancient Egyptians invent?

The Ancient Egyptians may have used the bow drill, but they didn't invent it. What other amazing things did this fascinating ancient culture completely fail to invent?

GUNPOWDER

The secret of gunpowder was discovered by the Chinese, some time in the ninth century AD. Not by the Ancient Egyptians, who gave up on weapons technology after the bow and arrow, choosing instead to invent mascara.

THE WHEELBARROW

As impressive as the pyramids are, they're even more amazing when you consider that they were built without using a single wheelbarrow, as the Egyptians didn't invent them. Credit for the humble wheelbarrow is again due to the Chinese, who invented them in the second century AD (although the Ancient Greeks may have had a go too).

THE VENDING MACHINE

If, after a hard day building the Great Pyramid of Khufu, you fancied a nice cold drink – well, tough. As an Ancient Egyptian, you were part of a culture that had completely failed to invent the vending machine. You may think this is unfair, but at least one other ancient culture managed to invent a rudimentary vending machine – the Ancient Greek engineer Hero of Alexandria describes a simple mechanism which would dispense holy water in exchange for a coin.

BOOKS

If you wanted to relax with a thrilling bestseller in Ancient Egypt, you'd have to make do with reading a scroll, or possibly a wall. Although the Egyptians made paper from papyrus, they never hit on the idea of putting leaves together to make books – a breakthrough made by the Romans some time later.

TOILET PAPER

Incredibly for a culture as sophisticated and paper-aware as the Egyptians, it didn't dawn on them to use paper for the most basic of chores. (Maybe papyrus wasn't the ideal paper for this, as it's tough and unyielding and only slightly better than the toilet paper you get in schools.) Instead, the first documented use of toilet paper is credited to the Chinese, in the sixth century AD (but neither culture invented an alarm system which tells you when the roll is running low).

(See also our feature on 'The Fascinating World of Concrete' for something else the Ancient Egyptians didn't invent. But might have done. Or might not.)

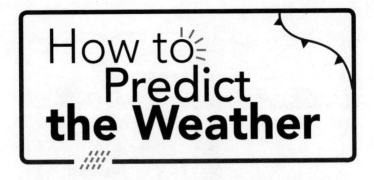

How to Predict the Weather

As we've discovered, modern urban man is pretty useless at dealing with nature. Take him out of his air-conditioned, temperature-controlled environment – take him on a camping trip, say – and he'll soon be reduced to a blubbering mess as there's no wi-fi and he can't get a skinny latte. Pretty soon he will start to notice that nature – red in tooth and claw, wild and uncontrollable – is all around him, and that it's dirty and full of insects.

We're going to help man once again claim his rightful place as master of his environment. And when it comes to the great outdoors, there really is no more immediate skill to learn than that of predicting the weather.

A piffling 86%

Weather forecasting is, even now, an imprecise science. Mathematically speaking, weather is a 'chaotic system', which doesn't mean that it can't be predicted, but does admit that the factors governing its behaviour are both colossally large and microscopically small, and interact in incredibly complicated ways. Even the experts at the Met Office only get it right 86% of the time (though admittedly that is quite high).

If they can't be relied upon absolutely, we have no choice – we're going to have to learn how to predict the weather ourselves.

Weather prediction – a brief history

Weather prediction is as old as humanity. Even primitive hunter-gatherers would have had their fortunes dictated to some extent by the weather, and would have had their own beliefs about how weather could be forecast.

The invention of agriculture, a system in which people are completely dependent on the elements, meant that the weather and weather prediction started to be taken very seriously indeed. The first

recognisable landmarks in the UK – the great stone circles at Avebury, Stonehenge and many other places – appear to have been built to calculate the seasons, with festivals like the Summer Solstice being roughly equivalent to our Bank Holiday.

(It's tempting at this point to imagine the Druids confidently predicting brilliant sunshine, and everyone heading off on a day out, only to end up sheltering under a dolmen, doing whatever was the historically appropriate substitute for watching *The Great Escape*, as it tipped it down. But I digress.)

For a few millennia afterwards, as rural communities became towns and cities, weather forecasting settled into a weird mish-mash of observation, superstitions and folklore of the 'cast ne'er a clout' variety. This era came to an abrupt end with the invention of modern meteorological science, which was (perhaps predictably, given the changeable climate of the British Isles) largely down to two Brits – Francis Beaufort and his protégé Robert Fitzroy, who in the nineteenth century introduced standardised measurements for most weather phenomena, such as gale force winds and clouds. Fitzroy headed the first incarnation of what would later become the Met Office.

Predicting the weather remains a serious business. For instance, in 2009, the town of Bournemouth claimed to have lost an alleged £1 million in tourism because thunderstorms were predicted for the May Bank Holiday – a day which turned out to be the finest and hottest of the year up to that point. It pays to get this stuff right.

Amateur weather forecasting

To sum up: weather is chaotic and massively complex, and even a highly skilled, multi-million pound enterprise like the Met Office still can't achieve a 100% success rate in predicting it. But we're not going to let these (admittedly huge and daunting) facts deter us. We're going to learn how to forecast the weather.

In order to make the most informed forecasts we can, we need to know everything we can about weather, beginning with the most basic question of all. What is weather?

Weather is the result of the day-to-day state of the atmosphere. Weather is driven by: the sun, atmospheric pressure, the interplay of warm and cold currents of air and the volume of water active within that system. This may seem like a vast and complicated subject, but it actually boils down to a few key things we need to know.

In order to predict the weather, we'll need to know about the following four basic things: Fronts, air pressure, wind and clouds.

Fronts – a rough guide

The place where two air masses meet is called a front, and these are the fronts they talk about on weather forecasts (and we all nod sagely and pretend we know what they are). Air masses and weather fronts are never static, and move and change all the time.

There are four types of front – warm, cold, occluded and stationary. Fortunately for us and our weather-predicting efforts, they all have distinctive effects which can help us predict *whether* they're on the way. All fronts, be they warm or cold, are associated with unsettled weather, plus old people looking sternly at the sky and talking nonsense about their bones.

WARM FRONTS
Created when a warm mass of air moves into a cold mass. Warm air is lighter, so the warm mass rises to cover the cold mass.
Tell-tale signs that a warm front's coming: The appearance of high Cirrus followed by lower, thicker Stratus clouds and then maybe rain or even, unless it's Christmas day, snow.
Warm Front weather: Warm air generally holds moisture collected from large bodies of water it's travelled over. As the warm air rises the moisture within condenses into droplets – a moment called 'the dew point' – and the water falls as rain or drizzle (usually on a bank holiday). Unlike a cold front, the passing of a warm front doesn't lead to clear weather, but spells of further drizzle in the cloudy, humid 'warm sector'.
On a weather map: A red line with regular red semicircles on it, indicating the direction it's travelling in, like so:

Do not adjust your book. These maps pre-date the invention of colour printing.

COLD FRONTS

Created when a cold air mass moves into a warm air mass. The warm air is lighter than cold air, so the cold air cuts underneath it.

Tell-tale signs that a cold front's coming: Showers and thunderstorms, and the formation of Cumulus clouds.

Cold Front weather: As cold fronts pass over, they bring a change in wind direction and a drop in temperature. As the cold front pushes warm air upwards, the moisture in the warm air will condense and fall as heavy, but short-lived, rain. Characteristically, the passing of a cold front delivers clear skies.

On a weather map: A blue line with regular blue triangles on it, indicating the direction it's travelling in, like so:

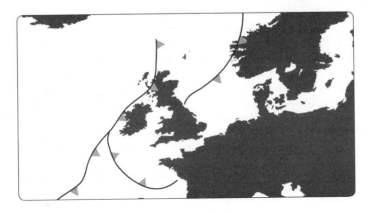

OCCLUDED FRONTS

Created when a fast-moving cold front catches up and combines with a warm front.

Tell-tale signs that an occluded front's coming: As an occluded front is basically a warm front merged with a cold front, it can exhibit the signs of both, beginning with those of a warm front. So the arrival of an occluded front is usually heralded by drizzly rain, followed by a downpour. As the front passes directly overhead, there'll be temperature and wind changes, after which the weather clears (as in a cold front), but still might be prone to spells of drizzle (as in a warm front).

Occluded Front weather: Warm front weather (drizzle, rain, etc) abruptly followed by cold front weather (a heavy downpour sometimes followed by clear skies).

On a weather map: A purple line with regular purple arrows and semicircles on it, indicating a fusion between the two different types of front we've already seen, like so:

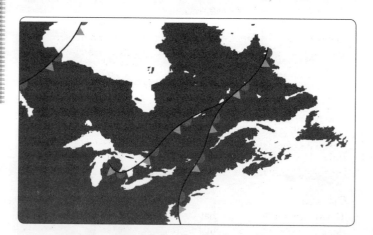

The last kind of front is a **Stationary Front** – an air mass, cold or hot, that isn't moving. Stationary fronts are associated with weak winds, rain and other kinds of precipitation.

Air pressure

The second thing we're going to need to know about if we're going to predict the weather is air pressure. Air pressure is a key factor in the creation of wind.

Briefly, wind comes about when air moves from areas of high pressure to areas of low pressure. As air rises in an area of low pressure, it creates clouds and rain and draws more air into the bottom of the low-pressure. The greater the difference between the two areas of pressure, the stronger and faster the wind it produces will be (but we'll deal with wind in slightly more detail in a minute).

Measuring the air pressure over a period of time should give us an indication of what the weather is doing – and, more importantly, what it might do later.

Wind

Wind can be a good indicator of what type of weather is on the way. Wind depends on specific barometric conditions, so as a general rule of thumb, wind from a certain direction will mean certain conditions can be expected (or are at least more likely).

That said, what type of weather the wind will bring depends on your geographic location. In the UK, the prevailing (or predominant) wind is south-westerly, and is coming in upwards from an ocean, after a long journey with very little variation in direction. As such, it brings us our unsettled climate of low pressure and their rain-bearing fronts, interspersed by fine spells with broken cloud and sunshine.

Find out what the prevailing wind is in your part of the world, and what kind of weather you can expect as a result. Using an anemometer and a weather vane or windsock, take readings over a period of weeks, and make observations about what kinds of weather come with winds from all points of the compass in your area.

Clouds

'Clouds symbolize the veils that shroud God' wrote Honoré de Balzac, which is lovely and poetic, but if we're being more scientific and brutal about it, clouds are condensed water vapour.

Generally speaking, the higher clouds are, the better the weather will be. Handily, storm clouds are usually dark grey or even black, and a more obvious indicator of impending bad weather you could not hope to find.

If you're going to learn to predict the weather properly, you'll have to know your clouds.

LOW CLOUDS – UNDER 7,000 FEET

 Cumulus Clouds – Puffy clouds, generally indicative of fair weather if they're small and widely spaced out. If they become big and tall, they can produce rain, and if they become large and bunch together, they can produce heavy rain, usually in warm weather. If they don't appear until the afternoon, fair weather is likely to continue. Cumulus, incidentally, is Latin for heap.

 Stratus Clouds – The grey skies common to the UK are usually made of low-lying stratus clouds, whose undersides clump together to form a layer ('Stratus' is Latin for blanket). If they lift and clear in the morning, this often indicates fine weather for the rest of the day. The classic 'cloudy day' cloud, their full name is the rather depressing 'Stratus Opacus Uniformis'.

 Stratocumulus Clouds – low-altitude masses of lumpy grey or white clouds – another grey sky cloud. They don't often produce heavy precipitation, and can indicate worse weather to come, but are just as likely to give way to clear skies. If they start to morph into Stratus clouds, this means rain is more likely.

MIDDLE CLOUDS – 7,000 TO 18,000 FEET

 Altocumulus Clouds – White clouds with patches of grey, they often appear in ripples. Considered to be fair weather clouds, they often appear after storms, but can also presage them. If they race across the sky and get thicker, this usually indicates rain is coming.

 Altostratus Clouds – Formless, ghostly grey-blue clouds that form a thin veil over the sky, through which the sun and moon will appear pale and watery. May eventually darken and thicken, obscuring the sun (or moon) and producing rain. They are formed by the rising and condensation of a large air mass, indicating an incoming front.

 Nimbostratus Clouds – Like altostratus clouds, but dark slate-grey in colour. They have a threatening appearance, and often bring rain or even snow that may last for several hours.

! *These symbols are only used on weather maps. You will never see them in the sky. If you do, call your nearest Met Office, and your doctor/therapist.*

HIGH CLOUDS – OVER 18,000 FEET

 Cirrus Clouds – or, more poetically, 'Mares' tails'. Cirrus only form at high altitudes, and are actually composed of ice crystals rather than water droplets. Often seen during fair weather, but can be indicative of fronts, especially if they start to clump together and thicken.

 Cirrostratus Clouds – More ice-clouds, these come in thin layers. Cirrostratus clouds produce a halo around the sun or moon, and are the only clouds capable of doing this, making them easy to identify. However, if a sky filled with Cirrus clouds gives way to Cirrostratus clouds, expect rain or snow.

 Cirrocumulus Clouds – Relatively rare layered clouds that produce the classic 'mackerel sky', resembling sand dune ripples or, indeed, the pattern on a mackerel's scales. They usually indicate fine weather.

 Contrail Clouds – Thin lines of vapour from jet engines that have turned into ice crystals, they also appear at this altitude.

TOWERING CLOUDS – IN EXCESS OF 50,000 FEET

 Swelling Cumulus Clouds – Swelling Cumulus clouds are typically flat-bottomed with growing cauliflower-like towers. Widely separated, they indicate fair weather, but bunched together they turn into many-headed monsters, and can bring on sudden rain. They can precede Cumulonimbus clouds, and often form in the heat of the day.

Cumulonimbus Clouds – Towering up to 50,000 feet high, these clouds bring most kinds of bad weather – rain, hail, sleet, thunder, lightning and, in extreme cases, even tornadoes. The top of the cloud is characteristically anvil-shaped. They are usually dark grey and angry-looking. They are the great white sharks, the T-Rexes, the Sherman tanks of the cloud world, and they bring the storm.

JAMES MAY

Home-made weather station

So now we have a basic understanding of four of the main climatological factors we should be looking out for. But if you're going to do this predicting-the-weather malarkey properly, you'll need to augment your data-gathering processes.

Considering your data-gathering processes are usually 'looking out of the window', we've a lot of ground to cover.

In order to get the best and most accurate readings possible, you'll need to assemble your very own Man Lab weather station. Instruments to help you forecast the weather are many and varied, and you should have a decent array of them to help you out.

Here are some of the basics. The more you can get your hands on, the more accurate your readings will be:

BAROMETER

A barometer measures changes in air pressure, which, as we've seen, indicate changes in the weather. There are two main types of barometer – the mercury barometer and the aneroid, or marine, barometer.

If your barometer is one of the slightly kitsch ones that has 'Wet' 'Fine' and 'Stormy' indications written in copper-plate on it, these readings are best ignored. A barometer only measures air pressure – it doesn't measure wind, humidity, temperature or cloud conditions, and as such is giving a very narrow-minded forecast. To get the best results from a barometer, use it to measure atmospheric pressure only, and then use that reading in conjunction with readings taken from the other equipment you have. This will build up a more accurate picture of the conditions you can expect.

The finer points of barometer reading would take up many pages, but for the moment suffice it to say that changes in barometric pressure are of more interest to you than whether the needle is pointing to 'Fine'. Changes indicate a variety of different things, so compare your barometer result with the other data you have for a better idea of what that result means.

As a general rule of thumb, a high reading means good weather and a low reading means bad. If the reading remains the same, conditions are likely to prevail. If the reading jerks and changes frequently, expect bad weather.

Of course, If you take regular readings with a barometer, you'll learn to 'read' the indications much better than these broad-brush indications.

Normal air pressure readings vary from 28 to 31 inches of mercury, which is the range given on most domestic barometers. Most professional meteorologists work in the much-more-precise millibars or hectoPascals. (One millibar/hectoPascal is roughly 0.0295 of an inch on a standard barometer, so let's stick to inches for the moment.)

TIP: If the thermometer and the barometer rise together, this is a very good indicator of fine weather to come.

TIP: Remember: Barometers are very sensitive to the air pressure above sea level. Adjust your barometer accordingly to get a precise measurement. Roughly speaking, one millibar should be added for every 30 feet above sea level.

ANEMOMETER

Measures wind speed. The most common type is the 'hemispherical cup' anemometer, designed by John Thomas Romney Robinson in 1846. Wind speed and pressure are closely connected, and changes in one will indicate changes in the other.

WIND VANE

Tells you from which direction the wind is blowing. Knowing where the wind is coming from can give you clues as to the temperature and the amount of water in the air moving into an area. If you can see a working weathercock from your weather station, this will also help.

THERMOMETER

Thermometers measure the air temperature, using the expansion or contraction of liquid or metal (usually alcohol or mercury) as a guide. You will probably already own one. Regular readings will help build up a picture of what type of air mass you are experiencing, and more pertinently, what that air mass is giving way to.

TIP: In winter, maximum temperatures occur between 1 and 2 pm, and minimum temperatures between 6 and 9 am. In summer, maximum temperatures occur between 3 and 4 pm, and minimum temperatures between 3 and 5 am.

TIP: To get the best picture of the day's temperature variations, take readings at 6 am, midday, 6 pm and midnight.

PSYCHROMETER

Or 'wet bulb thermometer' or hygrometer. Used to measure relative humidity. A psychrometer uses two thermometers, one bulb of which is covered with a wet cloth. As the cloth dries, the cooling effect of evaporation lowers the temperature on that thermometer. The rate at which this happens indicates the level of humidity in the air. Then the temperatures on the two thermometers are compared on a chart, thus giving the relative humidity.

RAIN GAUGE
Rain gauges are simple instruments used to measure the amount of liquid precipitation (or 'rain' as it's better known.)

The standard rain gauge, developed in the early twentieth century, is still the most common. It's basically a cylinder with a removable funnel. The funnel directs the rain into a collecting bottle, which is then measured. Readings are taken from the smaller, internal cylinder. It's this device that decides when we've had the 'X inches of rain' so beloved of TV newscasters.

There are many other instruments you could buy for your weather station – Thermo-hygrograph, anyone? – but the ones listed above are the most essential.

How to predict the weather
So – we've had a crash-course in climate, and we understand what different-shaped clouds mean. We've also got a variety of oddly shaped instruments to help us understand the weather better.

There remains but one thing to do.

It's time to predict the weather.

1. OBSERVE
Your first indicators are your senses. Look up at the sky, and take a few minutes to assess what you're seeing. Is it dry or wet? Warm or cold? Is there a wind?

2. FRONTS
Given what we now know about fronts, try to establish how these large-scale indicators of weather are behaving. First of all, establish whether the front is moving or stationary. If the front is moving, decide what type of front it is – a warm, cold or occluded front. Once you've done that, try and work out how the front is behaving – is it coming, or going? Is it breaking up and giving way to another front?

3. WHAT DO THE CLOUDS SAY?
What kind of clouds can you see? What are they doing? Establish what kind of clouds you're looking at, and what their behaviour is, then make

a judgement as to what this says about the weather moving in. As we've seen, clouds are enormously helpful, and can be a dead giveaway to the amateur weather forecaster.

4. TAKE READINGS
Check all the instruments you have to hand (don't fret if you've not been able to lay your hands on that thermo-hygrograph). What picture do their combined readings give? The more instruments you have, the more indicators you will have as to what the weather is likely to do.

5. REPEAT
In order to get the most accurate prediction, repeat all of the above at regular intervals throughout the day. No two days of weather are ever the same, and your readings and observations will change and reveal more throughout the day. Make observations over a few hours to give the best picture of what's happening to the weather.

6. ASSESS ALL DATA
Once you have all your readings, try and assemble the data into a coherent pattern. What does the data reveal? Larger trends like the arrival or departure of fronts should be relatively easy to assess, although it will be possible to make more detailed predictions based on your study of the clouds.

AND THAT'S IT.
You can now predict the weather. Never again will your barbecue be hastily relocated to your shed as you and your guests shelter from a horrendous downpour.

But can you escape from Dartmoor Prison, making your own way across acres of hostile and desolate moorland? And could you make and grow your own produce in your own home? No? Well, what about navigating using only some dodgy Elizabethan powder and an injured dog?

Fear not. By the time you reach the end of this book, you will be an expert in all these matters.

WEATHER FOLKLORE
TRUTH AND LIES

Everyone's familiar with 'Red Sky at night, Shepherd's delight: Red sky in the morning, Shepherd's warning'. (In fact, even Jesus knew that one, as he says in Matthew 16: 2–3 – 'When it is evening, ye say, "It will be fair weather: for the sky is red". And in the morning, "It will be foul weather today: for the sky is red and lowring"').

This saying is actually true. The dusk appears red because of dust particles pushed ahead of a high pressure system which is bringing dry air in with it. A red sky at dawn, meanwhile, means the impending arrival of a low pressure system bringing in moisture and possibly a storm.

But there are many other weather sayings, and not all of them are what you might call 'reliable'. Here are some old English weather ditties, along with the truth about how accurate they are:

'When March comes in like a lion, it goes out like a lamb. When it comes in like a lamb, it goes out like a lion'

March can indeed behave in both of these ways , but neither is a hard and fast rule. This saying does have a kernel of truth, however, as it acknowledges the changeable, capricious nature of March, when the sun moves northwards over the equator, and winter and spring are fighting it out for dominance.

'With dew before midnight, the next day will sure be bright'

Untrue. Dew occurs because of fine weather rather than signalling its arrival. So if there's dew, it's because the weather's already good.

'If the ash is out before the oak, you may expect a thorough soak'

Untrue. Oak trees will produce leaves before ash trees if the subsoil is wet enough. Not only that, there's another saying that indicates the exact opposite – 'If the oak is out before the ash, 'twill be a summer of wet and splash' – which makes all of this dubious at best.

'Rain before seven, clear by eleven'

Not strictly true. While as a general rule rain doesn't tend to endure for four continuous hours, it can rain intermittently all day. This maxim also seems to be truer in some areas than in others – there is a natural limit to the amount of rain produced in an area prone to low-pressure weather systems, meaning the weather might indeed clear by eleven, but this won't hold true for areas prone to high pressure systems.

'When trout refuse the bait or fly, there ever is a storm a-nigh'

The jury's out on this one. Some anglers swear that fish are more docile if there's a storm coming, with others insisting it makes no

difference. Rain reoxygenates water, though, and there's evidence to suggest that precipitation might cause certain kinds of flies to hatch, so there is at least a scientific reason for fish to become more active after rain. If you think you have a definitive answer to whether this is true or not, drop me a line. Or go on an Internet angling forum and argue about it.

'A fly on your nose, you slap, it goes; If it comes back again, it will bring a good rain'

True (incredibly). Flies tend to become more active and bother humans during periods of increasing humidity, which are usually indicative of imminent rain.

'When your donkey's leg falls off, spring will bring a cold and cough'

Alright, I made that one up.

CONQUER YOUR FEAR

A few generations ago, blokes were perfectly capable of fighting in wars, exploring the unknown or defending a lady's honour without a second thought. Modern man, however, appears to be scared of everything – clowns, spiders, commitment, dimly remembered 1970s public information films, flying, fighting, leaving a status update on Facebook that no one 'likes' . . . How has this sorry state of affairs come about? How have men ended up like this?

In researching this phenomenon, we made an even more staggering discovery – according to a recent study (conducted by us) 40% of men are scared of ghosts. Scared of something that probably doesn't even exist.

This was the final straw. We had to help the modern male locate his missing spine.

I got the fear

Franklin D. Roosevelt, in his inaugural address, famously observed that 'the only thing we have to fear is fear itself', but is this true? Is fear simply a state of mind, something that can be overcome by a highly trained and suitably stout-hearted individual? Or is it actually one of those biological responses we really should listen to?

Well, as in most things involving the human brain, yes and no – often at the same time. There are times when we should listen to our fight-or-flight responses, and other times when fear just makes a bad situation worse by clouding our judgement and magnifying tiny threats into huge, apparently immovable ones. It's a question of being able to control your fear, and make it work for you.

Whooooo

In order for you to control your own fear responses, and reclaim your bravado, I suggest you do something extreme – something that will test your nerves to breaking point. In fact, if modern men are so scared of ghosts, then facing that fear head-on and going ghost hunting would appear to be a great place to start.

Lots of haunted locations run organised ghost hunts, and some invite groups of people to stay overnight. That's certainly one way to do it, but to really test your nerves to the limit, and measure your fear responses, you can look into staying overnight alone somewhere (you can even get sponsorship to do this for some worthy cause).

Thus, your task is clear – in order to prove your worth as a man, you must find a suitable haunted house or castle and, once there, enter some of the darkest, scariest places in a place solely made up of dark and scary places, and then attempt to lower your fear to normal levels by using a series of proven fear-busting techniques.

Of course, if my prejudices on the matter of life after death and spectral visitors from beyond the grave are proved to be incorrect, and you do find yourself faced with beings of unspeakable evil from a realm beyond comprehension, the following fear-controlling techniques may be of limited value.

But there's really only one way to find out.

Ghost hunting – a noble pursuit (really)

In recent years, the noble pursuit of ghost hunting has, inexplicably, become a mainstay of various cable TV channels. In fact, the situation has become so bad that you can't channel surf for more than two minutes without coming across the familiar green resolution of a night-vision camera as it shows a screaming girl band attempting to stay calm in a medieval crypt. As a result of this, ghost hunting has acquired something of a tawdry reputation. This is a shame, as it is an old and illustrious pursuit.

Dealing with ghosts and spirits – and telling ghost stories – are ancient activities. One of the earliest accounts of an actual ghost hunt comes from Pliny the Younger, in AD 100. The story was old when Pliny retold it, and tells of a house in ancient Athens haunted by the ghost of an old man, and its subsequent investigation by one Athenodoros Cananites. When Athenodoros followed the ghost, it led him to a certain spot in the garden, where it promptly disappeared. Digging there, Athenodoros found human bones which he was able to bury properly, thus ending the haunting.

Interest in ghosts and spirits has always been with us, but enjoyed a boom during the Victorian and Edwardian periods, when spiritualism, table-rapping and ectoplasm became fashionable concerns. It was also during this period that formal investigation of ghost-related phenomena began. Ghost enthusiasts founded the Ghost Club in London in 1862, believed to be the oldest paranormal research organisation in the world. Famous members of the club have included Charles Dickens, and the renowned ghost hunter Harry Price.

And in the late 1960s, of course, a group of young kids in the USA specialised in tracking down ghosts with a Great Dane, though the ghosts in question often turned out to be the caretaker of the old mine/theme park/creepy house they were investigating.

Fear itself

Once you arrive at your designated haunted house, you can settle in for the night, unravel your sleeping-bag and steel yourself for a long night of bloodcurdling terror.

At this point, it's worth taking a minute or two to look at how fear works – how it's produced and how it affects us.

Fear is part of being human, and one of the oldest parts at that. Biologically speaking, its usefulness is obvious – it was only by being scared of leopards and tigers that our primitive ancestors successfully avoided being eaten by them. To this day, in fact, we still exhibit those same fears, for the exact same reasons. Phobias of things that might conceivably kill us (wild animals, heights, poisonous spiders) are far more common than more abstract fears such as clowns or the number 13. Or ghosts, come to that.

Fear is generated in the brain, and although the process is not fully understood, it largely involves a group of structures called the amygdalae, which process negative emotions. When a person is placed in a fearful or tense situation, activity in the amygdale increases and signals are sent to trigger the body's responses.

Fear has a very tangible and obvious effect on the body. The following are the body's classic reactions to fear:

Sweating – The production of sweat during fear is an ancient, animal response, designed to make you more slippery, and therefore more difficult for a potential threat to grab hold of.
Dilation of the pupils – When we're scared, the pupils of our eyes widen. This is another ancient evolutionary response designed to let in more light, enabling us to see better in the dark.
Adrenaline release – A hormone produced in the adrenal gland (situated just above the kidneys), adrenaline (or epinephrine) is released into the bloodstream and then rapidly distributed round the body,

increasing the heart rate and enabling us to use all our strength either to fight the threat or escape it (the famous 'fight-or-flight' reaction).

> **TIP:** Now might be a good time to work out your predicted maximum heart rate (roughly) using the following simple formula: 220 - Your Age = Predicted Maximum Heart Rate. If your ghost hunt goes badly, you might be exceeding it later on.

I ain't afraid of no ghost

Modern technology has transformed pretty much all traditional working practices nowadays, and even a hobby as weird and intangible as ghost hunting is not exempt from the microchip revolution. Indeed, the modern ghostbuster will be weighed down with a mind-boggling variety of devices and gizmos designed to help him detect the undetectable.

If you're serious about going looking for ghosts yourself, you might want to invest in any/all of the following:

- **Digital video recorder:** The cornerstone of any serious ghost investigation, enabling you to record any visual phenomena you encounter. Like most crucial tools, be sure you get a good one – preferably one with excellent sound.

> **TIP:** Make sure your camera has an infra-red function (as seen on every ghost TV programme of the last ten years). This will enable you to see obstacles, ghosts, Jodie Foster, etc in near total darkness. If you get scared, you can just pretend you're watching an episode of *Most Haunted*. Be warned though – most anecdotal ghost sightings take place in broad daylight.

- **Digital Camera:** A good digital still camera will enable you to zoom in and analyse any potentially paranormal happenings, provided you're not a trembling wreck by this point.
- **Traditional Camera:** In addition, you'll need a traditional film camera, which captures impressions in a different way to a digital camera. 35 mm is best. Take tons of spare film (and memory cards for the digital), just in case you hit the paranormal motherlode.
- **Traditional Analogue Tape Recorder:** Traditional magnetic tape is an excellent way of recording 'EVPs' (Electronic Voice Phenomena, or so-called 'Raudive voices') and other creepy sounds. Listen to the tapes afterwards – just because you didn't hear something first time doesn't mean it won't be on the tape, ready to crap you up when you listen to it some weeks later (a digital one is also acceptable, provided its range is good).

- **EMF Detector:** Some researchers claim that ghosts have a distinct and detectable electromagnetic trace. There's not much hard science to back this up, but it's certainly been established that weak magnetic fields can cause the brain to feel classic paranormal effects. An EMF detector will help you find these fields. Plus, it looks cool when you wave it about.
- **Thermal Imaging Camera:** Gives the 'thermal impression' of a room (and helps to establish where ordinary non-paranormal draughts are coming in).

On top of all that, you'll also need a compass, thermometer, barometer, torch, matches and candle, watch, motion detectors (or wind chimes, as a lo-fi alternative) and, if you're doing this with someone else, a walkie talkie.

Blimey. Alternatively, you could just take a crucifix and a Bible and hope for the best. Many ghost hunters get by with just a torch, a note-pad and a pen.

Controlling fear

For your ghost-hunting excursion, hardware is merely part of your armoury against the forces of fear. You should also arrive equipped with a battery of proven psychological techniques to help you keep calm.

The following methods are among the most well known for overcoming fear:

'Dutch courage'

This is not the kind of courage you have to summon up when you're boarding at Schiphol airport and you realise you haven't properly cleaned out your pockets after that stag trip to Amsterdam. No – this is the time-honoured tactic of dealing with fear by getting . . . well, pissed, basically. Unsurprisingly, it's an English invention.

During the Thirty Years War, English soldiers fighting in the Dutch Republic faced the twin evils of cold and the terror of impending battle. In order to protect 'our boys' in the seventeenth century from both of these evils, they were given rations of Dutch gin to keep them in fighting fettle, and the term 'Dutch Courage' stuck.

Drinking and fighting have gone together for thousands of years, however, and the Thirty Years War merely formalised the practice. By the time World War I came around, British soldiers were rationed two ounces of rum or a pint of porter daily, while their German adversaries got a pint of beer, half a pint of wine and a quarter pint of spirits. Eventually, drinking on duty became a problem for the authorities, with Chancellor of the Exchequer David Lloyd George moved to comment 'fighting Germans, Austrians and drink, as far as I can see the greatest of these foes is drink.'

There are very good scientific reasons for giving scared people a good, stiff drink. Alcohol dulls the senses, alters one's perception of situations and surroundings, affects memory and makes a person think he has more strength and skill than he really has. It also promotes aggression and makes a person rowdier. If you don't believe me, take a walk through your local town centre at 11.30 pm on a Friday night.

Sadly, although alcohol may reduce fear, it also reduces your competence when it comes to dealing with danger. So let's look at some other techniques.

'Flooding'

> *'I believe that anyone can conquer fear by doing the things he fears to do'* – ELEANOR ROOSEVELT

In ye olden days we used to call this technique 'facing your fears', but a more refined and extreme version of this is prevalent nowadays, and it's called flooding. Developed by Nicolas Malleson in 1959, and further refined by psychologist Thomas Stampfl in 1964, flooding exposes a scared person to a massive, prolonged hit of the thing they're terrified of. So, a person terrified of public speaking is given the mic at a stand-up comedy club, someone scared of spiders is locked in a tank with a hundred tarantulas, somebody with an intense fear of the way society is headed is made to watch *The X Factor*, and so on. An alternative version is 'implosive therapy' in which the phobic person is merely asked to consider the worst that can happen (or have it described to him by the therapist) until it loses its power to cause anxiety.

The idea of flooding is to exhaust the fear response – to make someone so scared they run out of reactions and are then able to treat the situation as if it's normal, and even comforting – to make the person realise that a place of safety can be found even in the midst of the very situation they dread.

Of course, all of this involves putting the phobic person through the most extreme distress imaginable in order to get results, which can be morally questionable. Psychiatrist Joseph Wolpe, in his book *The Practice of Behaviour Therapy*, describes an early experiment carried out by an unnamed physician to investigate the efficacy of the flooding technique. The physician took a subject – a woman who was afraid to travel in cars – and ordered her to be driven the fifty or so miles to his New York office, over several high bridges and through the two-and-a-half-kilometre long Holland Tunnel.

Needless to say, the woman – quite understandably – was half-crazed with fear for most of the journey, but eventually she realised the situation was actually manageable, and her fear hugely out of proportion to the actual danger presented, and thus she calmed down (the return journey provoked little or no reaction from the woman at all).

History doesn't record whether the unnamed doctor was subsequently arrested and imprisoned for arranging for a screaming girl to be driven around for hours against her will, but the point was proved.

So before embarking on any ghost hunt, you might want to get a friend with a creepy voice to read ghost stories to you for a while, or just simply watch *The Exorcist*. To do 'flooding' properly, remember to keep either activity up until you're as scared as you possibly can be, and then do it some more; and repeat, until being scared becomes ridiculous. It's only an ordinary household ghost for God's sake.

Keeping busy

'Inaction breeds doubt and fear. Action breeds confidence and courage. If you want to conquer fear, do not sit home and think about it. Go out and get busy'
— Dale Carnegie (author of How to Win Friends and Influence People)

One of the simplest ways of controlling fear is to do something else – a displacement activity that focuses your attention on practical things rather than running about and screaming. This is a good trick if *you* can do it, as it makes the fear incidental to getting on with something, and thus makes it controllable and manageable.

This technique received an unplanned field test in 2008, when a Soyuz descent module heading back to Earth from the International Space Station malfunctioned, forcing it into a dangerously fast and steep ballistic re-entry. During the subsequent, and potentially terrifying, course correction, astronaut Peggy Whitson claimed she was 'too busy to be scared'. (The craft eventually touched down safely in Kazakhstan, a mere 295 miles from its intended landing point.)

Yoga

Peculiar as it may seem in a manual such as this, aimed squarely at manning up the modern male and resisting all things both namby and pamby, we're now going to look at yoga as a manly method for controlling fear. This is not as odd as it may first appear – for much of its history, yoga was practised, recorded and developed mostly by men.

The 5,000-year-old practice of yoga has many functions, but most usefully for our purposes it helps to combine the best elements of some of the other techniques described here – relaxing the muscles, regulating breathing, and concentrating the mind on what the body is doing, which has the effect of bringing calmness. Yogic techniques such as meditation and disengagement from one's own thoughts are also useful in diverting terror. In fact, it was common for ancient yogis to find the most dangerous spots in the jungle or on mountain ledges to meditate, as overcoming the increased fear would lead to much deeper states of awareness than if practised in comfort and safety. So you're not the first.

There are many different types of yoga, but for the purposes of controlling fear, you're probably best off with Kundalini Yoga. Kundalini Yoga calms the body down by the use of controlled breathing, combined with body movement directed specifically at 'target areas'. Basically, what that means is that Kundalini Yoga aims to strengthen key areas of the body by charging them with oxygenated blood. This leads to better mental and emotional clarity, and enhanced resilience – invaluable in the fight against fear. (It also activates the coiled Kundalini energy or spinal fluid, stored at the base of the spine, which is then drawn up through the vertebrae and into the brain to access higher states of consciousness, and many other things beside – yoga is nothing if not a comprehensive system of philosophy.)

The only problem with this is that as yoga techniques go, Kundalini is quite advanced, and if you're reading this in your sleeping bag, in a haunted house, it's probably a bit late to learn it now. That said, some long deep breathing might be a good start.

Progressive muscle relaxation

Developed by American physician Edmund Jacobson in the 1920s, 'progressive muscle relaxation' (or PMR) is a technique for reducing fear and stress by alternately tensing and relaxing the muscles.

Here's how to do it:

- Focus your mind on a particular muscle group (either your face and head, your arms, shoulders and neck, your abdomen and chest, or your legs and feet).
- Inhale, then squeeze the muscles as hard as you can for about 8 seconds, making sure you feel the tension.
- After 8 seconds, suddenly let go.
- All the tightness and pain should then flow out of the muscles. Exhale as you do this to further the feeling of release.
- Relax in this way for about 15 seconds, then repeat the cycle again.

I fully acknowledge that it may be quite difficult to focus on this sequence if you're faced with a ghost or other terror from the beyond. But give it your best shot.

TIP: Say a cue word to yourself as you do the relaxation part of the exercise – repeating it later will help you to associate the word with a state of relaxation.

Breathing exercises

Deep breathing is a method of regaining control and managing the symptoms of anxiety and panic. It's particularly useful for the fear of flying.

One way of doing this is to place one hand on the abdomen and one on the chest, then focus upon trying to raise the lower hand and not the one on the chest when breathing (do it now – it's very effective).

Singing

Yes – singing. Singing may positively influence the immune system through the reduction of stress hormones. It'll also give you something to do.

Of course, it depends what you sing. In a tense situation, 'I Whistle a Happy Tune' from *The King and I* is probably better than 'Don't Fear the Reaper', or 'Ace of Spades'.

Civil conversation

Winston Churchill is, according to legend, responsible for a novel approach to fear, in a situation highly relevant to our current haunted house excursion.

Churchill stayed at the White House during World War II. After taking a bath he walked naked into the bedroom, and saw the ghost of Abraham Lincoln standing by the fireplace. Churchill remarked, 'Good evening, Mr President. You seem to have me at a disadvantage' – after which the spectral visitor disappeared. So, if you do see a ghost, remember to be courteous and polite.

Conclusions

After your (hopefully) non-nerve-racking night of non-terror at your chosen haunted location, you should come to the conclusion that fear is all in the mind, and can be conquered and controlled, and that there really is nothing to be scared of. Choose your fear-control technique wisely, use it well, and, when the time is right, you'll be a solid rock of sheer courage while those around you turn to jelly.

Only six hours to go till daylight.

'May I just offer a word of warning? One of the facts known about seeing a ghost is that if the witness has up to that time flatly refused to accept their existence, or has continually derided other people for believing in phantoms, he is likely to suffer a severe shock'
– ANDREW GREEN, GHOST HUNTING – A PRACTICAL GUIDE

JAMES MAY

FIVE VERY HAUNTED PLACES IN THE UK

Britain is reputedly the most haunted place in the world, a fact that used to be in the *Guinness Book of Records* until they realised how weird it looked. Here are some of the most haunted places in the most haunted place on Earth.

- **Hampton Court.** Even now, this Tudor stately home is crammed to the rafters with the unquiet dead. Catherine Howard, Henry VIII's fifth wife, visits the so-called 'haunted gallery' at Hampton Court, and the place is also home to the spirit of Dame Sybil Penn, who started haunting in earnest when her tomb was mucked about with in 1829. More recently, in 2003, CCTV cameras captured the image of a spectre opening a pair of fire doors at Hampton Court. The press dubbed the ghost 'Skeletor', due to his skull-like face, and the footage of his appearance became that week's worldwide Internet sensation.

- **Borley Rectory, Borley, Essex.** Built in 1863, the rectory had a history of haunting even before 1929, when ghost hunter Harry Price started the investigations that would make the house infamous. Debate still rages to this day as to whether Price was the most skilled paranormal investigator of the twentieth century, or a fraud who perpetuated the 'phenomena' at Borley himself. Nonetheless, Price wasn't the only person to witness psychic happenings at Borley, and many of the people who lived there had weird and terrifying experiences. The rectory itself burned down under mysterious circumstances in 1939, although some say that since then the paranormal happenings have simply transferred to nearby Borley Church.

- **The Tower of London.** Unsurprisingly, it is haunted by many of the famous people who were imprisoned there – including the ghost of Anne Boleyn – and is a strong contender for the title of 'most haunted building in the UK'. Intriguingly, the Tower is also said to be haunted by the ghost of a bear.

- **Glamis Castle, Glamis, Scotland**. Is there a mysterious secret room at Glamis Castle? Did said secret room once house a monstrously deformed member of the Bowes-Lyon family, hidden away from the world? Probably not on both counts, but it's a good story, and one that's still told to this day. Apart from this, the castle has at least three ghosts, most notably 'Earl Beardie', AKA Alexander, Earl Crawford, caught gambling on the Sabbath and condemned to play cards for all eternity.

- **Pluckley, Kent.** This quiet village in Ashford, Kent – which estate agents would no doubt describe as both 'sleepy' and 'leafy' – is home to at least twelve ghosts, and possibly as many as seventeen (estimates vary). Among the unquiet spirits of Pluckley are a highwayman, a gypsy, a schoolmaster, a colonel and monk, who, if they all appeared at the same time, might resemble a ghostly Village People tribute band.

WEIRD GHOST FACTS

- **Not all reported ghosts are of dead people** (contrary to popular belief). More than a few are apparitions of people who are still alive (though to be fair, the vast majority have kicked the bucket).

- **Ghosts aren't always people.** In fact, a vast range of phantom animals and objects have been reported over the years, ranging from horses, cats, dogs, a mongoose called Gef (at the famous 'Haunting of Cashen's Gap' in the 1930s), cars, trains and even planes.

- **Some ghosts seem to appear at moments of importance.** These are referred to as 'crisis apparitions'. The son who appears to his mother minutes before dying on the battlefield, the traveller who warns people away from a bridge which then collapses, and the dead spouse seen at the funeral of a loved one are all 'crisis' apparitions. Though as they all make suspiciously satisfying anecdotes, many researchers choose to see them as merely folk tales.

- **Most ghosts appear clothed.** This is interesting – if ghosts are supposed to be people's spirits, surely they don't need clothes? And if they do, why? Some people have suggested that ghosts

appear as they remember themselves in life, which begs all
sorts of questions. If you died in the 1970s, are you doomed to
wear brown corduroy flares for all eternity? Or can you change
your outfit? And, perhaps most philosophically interesting of all,
would the ghost of Rod Hull appear with or without Emu?

- **Ghosts might be recordings.** Although this was also the
  basis for a creepy 1970s TV movie (written by Nigel Kneale of
  Quatermass fame), the so-called 'Stone Tape' theory has been
  suggested in earnest by more than one researcher. The idea is
  that traumatic events are – by processes unknown – recorded
  in the stones and bricks of a building where unspeakable things
  have happened (prisons, asylums, the *Big Brother* house), and
  then play themselves over and over again, visible only to the
  'psychically sensitive'. As with most things ghosty, no conclusive
  evidence has yet been put forward.

Repair Shop

Open

Replacing a Tap Washer

A dripping tap can be a nuisance, and hiring a plumber for such a small job can be very expensive. However, there is an alternative – you can fix the tap yourself. Follow these handy illustrated instructions and say goodbye to dripping tap misery – forever.

If your tap drips when you turn it off, you need to replace the washer. If it's a basin or sink tap, you'll need a ½-inch washer, while bath taps usually require a ¾-inch washer. We'll have none of that 'metric' nonsense here.

Start by turning the water supply off at the stopcock. It's usually fitted on the mains supply pipe, where it enters the house. This is advisable for all domestic plumbing operations, unless a) you're Laurel and Hardy in their heyday, or b) your house is on fire. Open the tap to drain excess

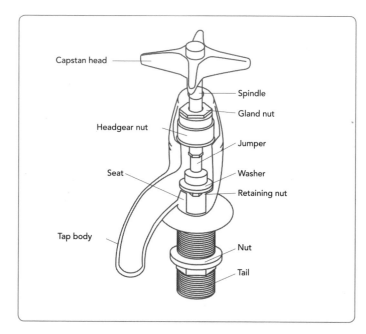

Capstan head

Spindle

Gland nut

Headgear nut

Jumper

Seat

Washer

Retaining nut

Tap body

Nut

Tail

water from the pipe. After a few seconds, the tap will empty and no more water will emerge. Remember to put the plug in the sink or bath. This will prevent the loss of any small parts down the plughole, and a subsequent Olympic-standard volley of swearing as you realise you'll have to dismantle the waste pipe to retrieve the missing part.

There are two main types of tap head – a capstan head and a shrouded head. A capstan head is yer classic tap shape, while a shrouded head is the kind that became more common in the 1970s.

The traditional tap is constructed as shown in the illustration above, where all the important parts are named.

For a capstan head tap, remove the capstan head by unscrewing the small screw on the base (this is the tap component voted most likely to go down the plughole). Then remove the tap cover, or shroud. You have now exposed the headgear, which holds the washer. Unscrew the headgear and remove the washer. Replace it, and then replace the headgear, the shroud and the capstan head.

For a shrouded head tap, the head should simply pull off to reveal the headgear, washer and nut, or it may be screwed on by a central screw, usually located in the centre of the tap (where the H or C indicator disc usually is).

With mixer taps, it's doubtful that both washers will have gone at once, so try and work out if the hot or cold side washer/ceramic disc has gone.

There aren't any washers or indeed a headgear inside a ceramic disc tap. Instead there's a cartridge containing two ceramic discs, each with two holes in. When the tap is turned, the discs align and water flows. If these discs wear down, the tap will leak.

That's all the major types of tap covered, you'll be relieved to hear.

Worth knowing: If water oozes up around the spindle of the tap, you probably don't need to replace the washer at all. Just tighten the gland nut on the headgear by about half a turn or so.

Job's a good 'un!

> **TIP:** Ceramic taps can also leak because gunk gets between the sliding faces. Any amount of tightening the central screw won't stop a leak if the faces are dirty, so check they're clean. This applies especially in hard water areas, where limescale builds up.

TIP: When turning any nut on a tap, take care not force it, as the entire tap assembly could turn, damaging the pipes. If you have to give it some welly, brace it with your hands or a piece of wood.

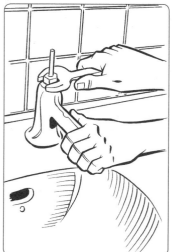

TIP: If the tap cover, or shroud, doesn't want to come off, gently blow some air from a hot air gun lightly around it (though this is not recommended for plastic sinks and baths).

TIP: Modern taps have an O-Ring instead of a packing gland. While the tap is dismantled, check the O-Rings. If they're worn, prise them off with a flat-bladed screwdriver, and fit new ones. O-Rings cost much less than new ceramic cartridges.

*Just say you're fixing the taps in Peter Stringfellow's house, for instance.

Quick Tip

Steak and Wine ✓

Imagine the situation – you've got someone you fancy coming round for dinner in 20 minutes. You've promised to serve them steak cooked to perfection, and serve it with a bottle of fine wine.

Trouble is, despite having eaten tons of the stuff, you've never cooked steak before – and certainly not for anyone who might be fussy about *how* it's cooked. To add to your troubles, your one-and-only corkscrew breaks and there isn't time to buy a new one. You're trying to impress this person and you're about to serve two slabs of raw or possibly burnt meat and an unopenable bottle of wine. Things are looking grim.

Fortunately, you own the Man Lab manual you now hold in your hands and victory can be snatched from the jaws of a Chinese takeaway. Here we present a very quick guide to cooking the perfect steak, and opening a bottle of wine toollessly.

Cooking the perfect steak:

As anyone who's eaten in more than two restaurants knows, it can be very hard to get a properly cooked steak. Steak-cooking is a delicate art, and it may seem that most of the regular cookbook instructions on how to cook steak vary, or are imprecise. Fortunately, you have a natural indicator of how long to cook meat for right in front of you. Your hands.

How to tell if a steak is cooked the way you intended it to be, using your hands:

Meat is muscle, and as such behaves in a fairly predictable manner when tensed and relaxed – and, helpfully for us, when cooked. With that in mind, hold up your hands and I'll show you how to measure accurately how cooked your steak is.

Rare (see illustration opposite):
Open your left hand as shown.
Touch the tip of your index finger to the tip of your thumb.
Now, with your right hand, pinch the web of muscles* between the thumb and the rest of your hand. They will now be at exactly the same consistency as a perfect rare steak.

*Your Adductor pollicis muscles, to be precise.

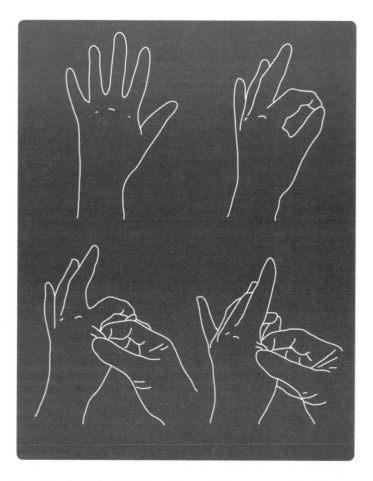

Repeating the trick with different fingers will give you a good guide as to how cooked your steak is, like so:

Medium rare – middle finger

Medium – well-done – ring finger

Well-done – little finger

Now, using the above guide, cook that steak, poking it ocassionally with a forefinger to test its consistency.

The steak-hand trick means you now have a rough guide to getting the meat to the right consistency. For all but the most discerning dinner guest, this should see you right. Be careful not to cook your hand and squeeze the steak, by mistake. Also, remove oven gloves.

Cooking the steak to *absolute* perfection, however, is a highly complicated business that chefs take years to learn. Below are some general tips that will make for a better steak:

- Always buy good meat. Ideally, steak meat should be hung for 21 days. When choosing a steak, look for 'marbling' in the meat, which indicates the presence of fat. This should impart a nutty taste to the steak.
- Cook the meat from room temperature, rather than refrigerated. Even better, 'relax' the meat for eight minutes before cooking; this is done by putting the steak in the oven on the lowest possible setting, with the door slightly open.
- Always use tongs to turn the meat to avoid piercing it and losing the precious juices within.

Opening a wine bottle without a corkscrew

OK, that's the steak problem solved. All that leaves us with is the problem of opening our bottle of wine. Here's how:

You Will Need
- A towel (or a phone book)
- A vertical surface (a wall or a tree)
- To have removed the foil from the top of the bottle
- To have checked that it isn't a screw-top

Place the towel (or phone book) at the base of the bottle to cushion it. Now, with what we can best describe as 'considered force' (i.e., hard enough to work but not hard enough to smash the bottle), bash the base of the bottle against the surface (see opposite):

The banging should ease the cork out bit by bit. Repeat until you can easily twist the cork out with your fingers. Now answer the door. Your guest has arrived – none the wiser to your pre-dinner traumas.

TIP: Use a sturdy wall, rather than a plasterboard stud wall. (Although a yawning hole in your wall might provide an amusing conversation piece during dinner, and a suitable distraction from your rotten cooking.)

tool of the week:
the hammer

Can you knock in a nail? Or, like most men, do you just think you can? We'll find out as our toolkit tour continues with the cornerstone of any decent toolkit – the hammer.

The hammer appeals to us on a very basic level as its function is so pure and obvious – it's for hitting things with. But if you were to assume that was all there was to it, you'd be wrong, as anyone who's ever tried to knock a nail in (or pull out a hopelessly bent one and start again) will testify. Using a hammer properly takes skill.

Hammer basics

The hammer is one of the earliest known tools. It's been in use in one form or another for as long as there have been people (and before that – even today, primates can be observed using stones and wood to hammer open nuts). But even if we're being strict, and defining a hammer as the classic T-shaped object consisting of a handle and a striking head, the hammer is still incredibly ancient and has been in use since the Paleolithic or Stone Age, 30,000 years ago. The hammer's as old as humanity.

Hammers you need

There's a variety of hammers, but the main one you'll need for home DIY is the good old . . .

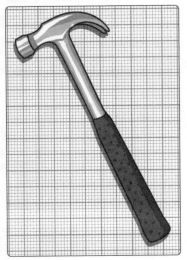

Claw hammer: An essential part of any toolkit – the sergeant major, if you will. A versatile tool that isn't just for knocking nails in – it's for taking them out too, with the 'claw' lever on the other side of the head. It's also ideal for knocking in a great variety of nails, from large cut and wire nails to galvanised clouts and tacks. When it comes to pulling out nails, a hammer with a curved claw is better than a hammer with a straight claw, as it has more leverage.

No other hammer is quite as important as this one, but it's helpful to have a variety of them on hand for other jobs. Other hammers you might want to invest in include:

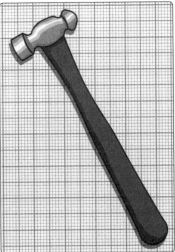

Ball-peen hammer: One of a family of 'peen' hammers (or 'pane' or 'pein' – spellings vary), useful for driving in smaller nails and tacks. 'Peening', by the way, is the process of working a metal's surface to enhance its material properties, which is what the ball head is for, though it's also good for flattening rivets, should the need arise.

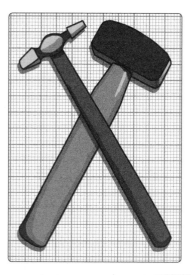

Pin hammer: Or tack hammer. For driving in the smallest panel pins or tacks.

Lump hammer: A squat-looking, no-nonsense hammer for driving chisels or bolsters into stone, and (as its appearance would suggest) 'light demolition work', i.e., smashing stuff up.

TIP: Don't forget to purchase a nail punch as well – basically a short pen-sized metal rod with a plastic handle surrounding it. This handy piece of equipment is used for knocking the nail head flush with, or beneath, the wood surface. It can then be filled and painted to make the nail invisible.

TIP: There are other tools available for removing stubborn nails from wood, in addition to the claw on the claw hammer's head – a nail puller or cat's paw is among the best. Another method for extracting particularly stubborn nails is to use an old pair of pliers or pincers, though try not to twist the nail as some are liable to snap.

Hammer prep

All hammers are not created equal. Claw hammers tend to come in a weight range of between 10 and 20 ounces, so when buying a claw hammer, choose one with the right weight for you. Go on – heft it a bit first. This is worth doing, as it's likely to be the tool you'll be using most.

TIP: Use the right hammer for the right job. Most especially, don't use your beloved claw hammer for jobs that would be better suited to a lump hammer – i.e., smashing stuff up.

Using the hammer

Some hammer techniques come instinctively, but most will come with practice. The basics of knocking a nail in accurately are very simple, but even the professionals manage to cock it up every so often. Using the thumb and index finger of the hand you use the least, hold the nail at a 90 degree angle to the surface you're nailing into, and strike the head of the nail firmly and evenly with the hammer (held in the hand you use the most), keeping your wrist straight.

You can read about this as much as you like, but the only way to really get good at knocking a nail in is to do it again and again, until you 'feel' the correct way to do it, and it becomes instinctive.

> **TIP:** Select the right nail. The importance of this cannot be underestimated. Using the wrong nail – hammering oval wire nails into brick, say – is not just a waste of time, it's also an excellent way to hurt your wrist. There are many types of nail, so make sure you know which are which and what they're used for.

Top Jobs for Hammers

- Knocking in nails (and pulling them out)
- Knocking in rawl plugs (both plastic and wooden)
- General knocking things together (and apart)

Hammer safety

Obviously, be very careful when knocking in nails with a hammer. Hitting your thumb (and then watching it turn red and start to throb painfully) might sound like something from a cartoon, but it's considerably less hilarious when it happens to you.

Never leave a hammer (or indeed any tool) at the top of a stepladder, where it can easily be forgotten about. You will remember it when you move the ladder and it falls off and smacks you on the head.

> **TIP:** If you're hammering or drilling into a lath and plaster or plasterboard wall (say to hang a picture), be extremely careful not to hit any water or gas pipes or electricity mains. Use a stud locator. These handy devices will tell you where the wooden uprights or 'studs' are in your wall.

> **TIP:** A hammer needs very little maintenance – it's a hammer – but you may want to occasionally run a metal file along the blades of the claw to refine the edge that will grip the shanks of nails.

Famous Hammers in Rock and Pop

Maxwell's Silver Hammer

Fictional nail-knocker-inner and murder weapon on the Beatles' *Abbey Road* album. McCartney wrote it, and Lennon hated it. Recording it apparently took ages, too.

MC Hammer

Sadly non-fictional massive-trousered rap 'MC' of the early 1990s. Has since done the decent thing and vanished without trace, but his huge hit 'U Can't Touch This' sadly hasn't, and can still be heard at wedding receptions, school discos, etc.

Hammer of the Gods

Not an album, or a single, but journalist Stephen Davis's warts-and-all biography of Led Zeppelin, published in 1985. Contains several infamous stories of the Zep's jaw-dropping off-stage antics, the accuracy of which the band themselves have contested.

Sledgehammer

Massive 1980s hit for Peter Gabriel, renowned for its groundbreaking claymation video. Nick 'Wallace and Gromit' Park animated the frozen chicken segment, fact fans.

Hammersmith Apollo
(formerly Hammersmith Odeon)

Legendary rock venue from the 1960s onwards, immortalised in the title of Motörhead's *No Sleep 'Til Hammersmith* album of 1981 (Even though the album wasn't recorded in Hammersmith, or anywhere near it).

The Army of Claw Hammers
in Pink Floyd's 'The Wall'

D'you know what? I don't think Roger Waters had the best time at school. Just a guess.

PRISON BREAK

There are many guides for men that tell you how to break out of prison. So many, in fact, that I'll wager an ounce of 'snout' that, by now, most blokes between the ages of 15 and 65 are *au fait* with every prison-break technique in the book. We all know the basics – nicking a guard's uniform, climbing into a wicker laundry basket, tunnelling through the wall over a period of 25 years using a geology hammer – and they're starting to get a bit over-familiar. Especially with the guards.

What these guides don't tell you is what to do afterwards. It's no use staging a flawless escape if you get put back inside 20 minutes later because your orienteering skills are non-existent, or you've disguised yourself very badly as a farmer's daughter.

So – we're not going to teach you how to escape from prison. But we are going to teach you how to *stay* escaped. Specifically on Dartmoor.

'I can hear the hound dogs on my trail, all hell breaks loose, alarm and sirens wail...' – THIN LIZZY, JAILBREAK

Staying escaped

Let's say you've tunnelled out of the exercise yard, scaled the 15-foot-high wall, evaded the searchlights and now find yourself in the middle of Dartmoor. Then what? You're in open country, miles from anywhere. In order to make good your escape, you must make it back to civilisation – and you must do so without being captured.

The trouble is, pretty much every bit of Dartmoor looks like pretty much every other bit of Dartmoor. You've no way of knowing where you are, which way is north, what time of day it is or whether it's best to evade capture by running as fast as you can or furtively sneaking across the landscape.

Some men would no doubt panic at this point, but not you. You're cool-headed, calm and in control. You have a compass and a map that you very thoughtfully got your contacts on the outside to smuggle into prison for you, inside a Battenburg cake. And what's more, you bought this book some time ago and have committed the following information to memory.

Cunningly, you've also timed your escape to happen during summer, when foliage is full, providing maximum coverage, and the ground is firmer and drier, meaning you will leave fewer tracks.

Still, they're on your tail already, so you'd best get moving.

The first few minutes

'If I stay in one place I can hardly think at all'
— *JEAN-JACQUES ROUSSEAU*

The first thing we need to do is get away from the scene of the escape (i.e., the prison itself) – and quickly. But how do we know we're going in the right direction?

The short answer to that is, we don't, but we can deal with the tricky matter of orienteering in good time. Initially, the most important thing in any good jailbreak is to get out of the area quickly, and put some distance between yourself and your pursuers. Then, after you're satisfied that this has been achieved, slow down, find cover, take some time to think about your predicament, and plan your next move. Remember – running and fast movement create more clues, signs and signals, and therefore make you easier to track, so be wary. You'll also create more noise and tire more easily.

Done that? Good. You should now be some distance from the prison, moving at a slow, steady pace, albeit in an unknown direction. It's time to find out where you are, and where you're going.

Out on the wily, windy moor

Dartmoor is currently a category 'C' prison – for prisoners who cannot be trusted in open conditions but who are unlikely to try and escape. The main body of the prison was built between 1806 and 1809, and was originally for housing prisoners brought back from the Napoleonic wars. The prison has a long and interesting history, which means that unlike most houses of correction, it has a museum and gift shop.

Although Dartmoor isn't the inescapable Alcatraz-like fortress of popular mythology, it does boast one security feature that gives it an undeniable edge – the miles and miles of desolate moorland surrounding it.

If you're going to make good your escape, you will have to find your way across this bleak and lonely wilderness unassisted.

Dartmoor Facts

- Despite being mostly moor, Dartmoor National Park is home to about 33,000 people (although estimates vary), roughly the same as the population of Cleethorpes.

- Dartmoor covers 368 square miles.

- There are bogs on Dartmoor. The most notorious of these is Fox Tor Mires, said to be the inspiration for the Great Grimpen Mire in Conan Doyle's classic *The Hound of the Baskervilles.* The fearsome reputation of most of them is undeserved, but nonetheless – all peat bogs should be treated with caution.

- Peat bogs on Dartmoor are created by layers and layers of sphagnum moss and other vegetation decaying into peat. While most bogs are shallow and are an annoyance rather than a mortal danger, peat bogs are still best avoided. If you do get into trouble, there'll be no one to help you. Steer clear of any areas of bright green bog moss, even if they lie right across your path. Proceed with caution in any boggy area.

- Dartmoor's weather is extremely changeable, and among its most notorious weather patterns are patches of dense low-lying hill fog which can form extremely quickly. If you get stuck in one of these, it may be advisable to stay put until it lifts, rather than losing your way and your bearings entirely. Your pursuers will be similarly befogged, so you're both in stalemate until the mist lifts.

JAMES MAY

Which way?

So we know roughly where we are, but which way are we headed? We need to get our bearings, and fast.

Establishing the compass points

There are several main ways of doing this:

1. THE 'SHADOW TIP' METHOD

- Find a straight-ish stick about a metre long. Straighter the better.
- Find a level patch of ground. Jam the stick upright in the ground.
- Make sure it's secure and unmoving as it's going to be there for a while.
- Mark the end of the shadow that the stick casts with a stone. Handily, this point will be west anywhere on earth (making this the handiest tip in the entire book, bar the ones in the fish finger sandwich chapter).
- Wait about 10–15 minutes until the shadow moves and mark the new location of the shadow tip with another stone. The new stone marks east. Draw a straight line between the two points.
- You now have a line with 'West' at one end of it and 'East' at the other. With west on your left and east on your right, you can draw another line midway through (and at right angles to) your original line, to give you north and south.

Disadvantages: The method described above works well near the middle of the day all year round, but will be substantially inaccurate early or late in the day in the summer or winter. Using this method means you have to stop for at least 15 minutes to get a reading. You'll also leave behind many tell-tale clues that you'll then have to waste more time disguising. It also only works if it's sunny.

2. THE 'WATCH METHOD'

- Take off your watch. Hold the watch horizontally, and arrange it so that the hour hand is pointing at the sun.
- Imagine a line between the hour hand and 12 o'clock. This is your north/south line.
- Now face north. West is on your left and east on your right.

Disadvantages: You'll need a watch in the first place, and a non-digital one at that. Plus, this is another method where you'll need sunshine, which on Dartmoor may not be forthcoming. The method as described above only works for the northern hemisphere, which is good for Dartmoor, but not much use on 50% of the planet (though frankly, if you don't know which hemisphere of the planet you're on, finding the points of the compass is the least of your problems). If your watch is set to British Summer Time, it will make your readings much less accurate.

3. THE 'CELESTIAL METHOD'
- Look up at the night sky.
- Find the constellation Cassiopeia. Cassiopeia is a rough 'W' shape, and is fairly prominent in the night sky.
- Then, find the Plough (or 'Big Dipper', if you're in North America. Or 'Saptarshi' if you're in Asia).
- If you imagine a line from the last star of the Plough, following the same angle set by the star behind it, and another line directly below the central star of the W in Cassiopeia, they meet at Polaris – the North Star, or Pole Star. Handily for the human race, the North Star is less than 1 degree off true north, and, from our earth-bound perspective, does not move because the axis of the earth is pointed towards it.

Disadvantages: For this method to work, it needs to be a clear night. Most people aren't confident astronomers, and it's possible (though difficult, admittedly) to get the wrong constellations. This is another method exclusive to the northern hemisphere.

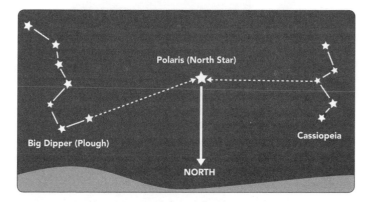

Polaris (North Star)

Big Dipper (Plough)

Cassiopeia

NORTH

TIP: Navigating by the stars is easier than you might think, and definitely worth learning if you're serious about orienteering/breaking out of Dartmoor. Of the 5,000-odd bright stars visible to the naked eye, fewer than 60 are used by navigators, making stellar navigation considerably easier to learn and memorise than stellar astronomy.

The 'Horns' of the moon

If you're travelling at night, (and it's clear, and the moon's up, and it's in the right phase), the moon can also be used to determine your direction. An imaginary line drawn from the 'horns' (points) of the waxing and waning moon down to the horizon gives a rough indication of where south is in the northern hemisphere (and where north is in the southern hemisphere).

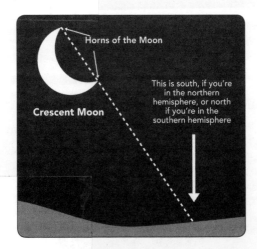

Horns of the Moon

This is south, if you're in the northern hemisphere, or north if you're in the southern hemisphere

Crescent Moon

4. BUILD YOUR OWN COMPASS

- Take an ordinary sewing needle. Polarise the needle by stroking it on a piece of silk or, if you've forgotten to pack an immaculate square of silk during your prison break, your hair. Only stroke in the one direction otherwise the needle won't polarise correctly.

- Dangle the needle from a thread tied halfway along its length. The needle should now point north.

> **TIP:** The needle will give a better reading if it's put on a piece of paper or a leaf and floated in water, but this will take slightly longer to organise. Don't lose the needle.

Disadvantages: You'll need a needle and, ideally, some silk, both of which you may not have (and won't be able to pick up, in the middle of nowhere). Polarising the needle correctly takes valuable time. If you're bald, polarising the needle on your hair is not an option.

> **TIP:** Worth knowing – some rocks on Dartmoor are magnetic, and will throw any compass off if you get too close to them.

Worth knowing if you're not on Dartmoor:
- The shadow-tip method isn't much use in the polar regions, which are latitudes above 60° in either hemisphere.
- The watch method isn't much use in lower latitudes, particularly below 20° in either hemisphere.
- The North Star gets higher in the sky the further north you go, and therefore isn't much use after about 70° N latitude.

Pick one of these methods and establish the points of the compass.

Alternatively, if you managed to get hold of a compass in prison, just look at that.

Crossing the landscape
Directions established, you're on the move again, and you now know where you're going. But your problems aren't over yet.

If you've escaped from Dartmoor, it's best to assume that the authorities will not simply call it quits and let you off. They will be coming after you. You will have to know how best to traverse the terrain around you to remain hidden and evade capture.

The following are good general rules for traversing your environment while minimising your chances of being detected.

OPEN AREAS

The best way to avoid detection in open areas is to avoid them, if at all possible, and find an alternative route. If this isn't possible don't just blunder across and hope – watch the area first from a safe position, to see if it's being patrolled or monitored. It's best to discover this now, rather than in the middle of open country with no hiding place. If there are fields, stick to the edges and hedgerows. Don't cut through high grass if possible, as you'll leave a very obvious trail for others to follow.

Finally, cross the area as quickly as you can – don't attempt to disguise your tracks or anything fancy like that in open country, as this will prolong the time you're exposed.

CROSSING A TRAIL

If you come across a path or trail, extra care is required. Any pathway will probably be used by your would-be captors, and they will notice any tracks or traces that you leave. So, try to enter a trail where the ground is hard, so you won't leave tracks. If this isn't possible, then try and disguise your tracks, but be careful – poorly disguised tracks are just as obvious as undisguised ones. If the trail or path is narrow, step over it altogether.

When entering and exiting a track, leave the vegetation as you found it. Apply the same rules to crossing roads, but be extra-vigilant as these are more likely to be watched.

STREAMS AND RIVERS

Much like crossing a track or trail, you're best off fording a stream or river at a place where the bank is firm, thus minimising the tell-tale scuff marks that indicate someone's got in or climbed out. Don't slide down the bank on the way in, as this is tantamount to painting a big arrow on the bank and writing 'He went thataway'. Be careful on exiting the river or stream as you're probably now dripping wet, and this will leave a trail. Try and shake off the excess moisture before you leave, but do this in such a way that you leave as little trace as possible. Generally, you should avoid attempting to cross rivers as they can be extremely dangerous (for more on this, see p.139).

On places like Dartmoor, where treacherous hazards such as bogs and dense undergrowth abound, skirt round them instead of attempting to battle your way through them. In general, obstacles such as these are more common at the bases of valleys, so keep to the higher ground if possible.

Counter-tracking – the sneaky art of survival

In addition to all the orienteering you'll have to do, you'll also have to be cautious, wily, and in some instances downright sneaky to throw your pursuers off your scent. In order to do that, you're going to have to learn and employ some basic counter-tracking techniques.

Here are some of the most reliable:

BACKWARD WALKING

This is one of the simplest and most effective ways of throwing someone off your trail. Retrace your footsteps by carefully walking backwards, treading into the tracks you've already made and matching them exactly (the longer you're able to do this for, the more confusing it will be). Then, simply step off your trail, into terrain that leaves little trace of your actual trail, such as rocks or harder ground, and continue on your way. With luck, your pursuer will continue to follow your dead-end false trail for no short while, buying you some time. If you're very lucky, this manoeuvre may even give your pursuers the slip completely.

JAMES MAY

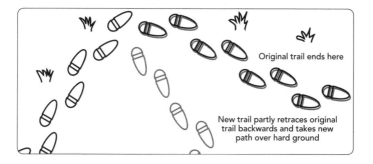

Original trail ends here

New trail partly retraces original
trail backwards and takes new
path over hard ground

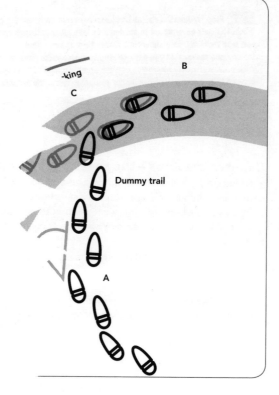

'T THE CORNER'

...proaching a well-worn road or trail that
...n, use this to your advantage. As you approach
... degrees toward it, away from the direction
... make your way a little way down the
...ous and easy-to-follow trail (B). Then retrace
... the point where you joined the trail (C). Then,
... from that point, creating as weak a trail as
... in the direction you intended to go (D).
...most likely follow the obvious trail in the belief
...e corner. This method can also be used at streams

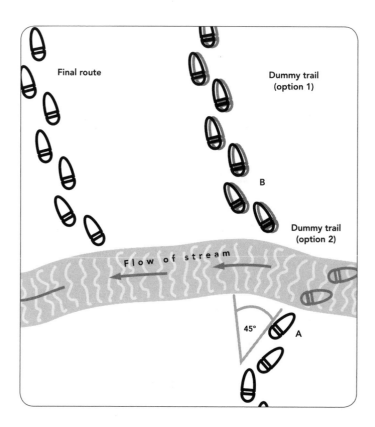

Final route

Dummy trail
(option 1)

B

Dummy trail
(option 2)

Flow of stream

45°   A

RIVERS AND STREAMS

Rivers and streams can be used in much the same way as trails and
roads in the method detailed above – with the added advantage
that you won't leave tracks. So, do your 45-degree entering-the-
river bit, making them think you've waded upstream (A), or just get
out and create a dummy trail for a short way, and then backwards-
walk your way back to the stream (B). You can then wade to
the point where you genuinely are going to exit the stream. If
your point of exit is downstream, then so much the better – the
flowing water will erase evidence of you leaving, and there may
be tributaries you can wade along and climb out of, throwing
your pursuers off the scent still further. Needless to say, caution is
advised with rivers and streams, and none of the above is possible
with a large, fast-flowing river.

USE TREES

A variation on the above techniques is to use a tree to mask your actual trail – the bigger the better. After you've passed a large tree, make a false trail for a distance, then carefully backwards-walk your way back to the tree. Then make your way around the trees, taking care to leave as little indication as possible of your presence on the genuine route. With any luck, the tree should hide your real trail and your pursuer will follow the false one.

> **TIP:** It's worth taking some time to destroy some of your tracks, just to increase your chances of a clean getaway. With a stick, erase a portion of your tracks as you go. Cover the mess with topsoil or leaf matter to further muddy the picture. Beware though: a badly disguised track won't fool anyone and will cost you valuable minutes.

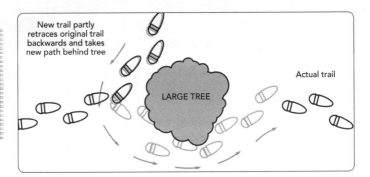

New trail partly retraces original trail backwards and takes new path behind tree

Actual trail

LARGE TREE

> **TIP:** Change footwear if possible, or wear your socks over your shoes, thus reducing and altering any footprints, and confusing your pursuers. You can put them back on the right way when you've made it to civilisation.

These techniques will not guarantee you will make good your escape to freedom, but they certainly won't hurt your chances. Remember – the people tracking you will be professionals. They will know what to look for, so do not underestimate them, or assume that your ruses have always been successful.

> **TIP:** Carefully stepping from stone to stone or stump to stump will leave the fewest traces of all, so do this wherever possible.

Natural signs

There's one more set of tips that will be of use in your escape to victory. The natural world and the landscape can be enormously helpful when it comes to doing a runner. You can even use nature to establish the points of the compass if there's no sunlight, it's not night and you haven't got a watch or a needle. Or you do have a needle, but you're bald.

The landscape bears the signs of the forces that work upon it, and these are evident in ways both big and small.

PATHS, PLANTS AND PUDDLES

In the northern hemisphere, the sun spends most of its time in the southern half of the sky, and this shows in many different ways. A path that runs east–west will get more sunlight on its northern (south-facing) verge, and there may well be more vegetation on that side. Also, it will have fewer puddles on that side, as there's more sun to dry them out. A path that runs north–south receives the same amount of sunlight on both sides, so in theory the amount of vegetation and the amount of puddles will be the same both sides.

TREES

This bias in the northern hemisphere towards southern sunlight is also apparent in trees. Trees often exhibit a heavier level of growth on their south-facing side in order to maximise the amount of sunlight absorbed, and this can be an easy indicator of south and north. This trait is easiest to find in isolated deciduous (leaf-shedding) trees. Be warned when using this method, however, as tree growth is dictated by many other things, not least of which is exposure to the wind. Thinner trees such as alder and poplar tend to lean towards the sun.

If a tree has recently been felled, you can 'read' the stump – the heart of the wood (the innermost rings, often a different colour to the outer rings) will usually be closest to the south side.

JAMES MAY

Cheating

Of course, if you find yourself near a town, there are several very obvious non-natural tips which will tell you at a glance which direction you're travelling in.

Tennis courts: these are usually laid out on a north–south alignment to avoid the players squinting into the sun. Cricket pitches are usually oriented the same way, and for the same reason.

Graveyards: Christian graves are usually laid out on an east–west alignment, as are churches. This is in accordance with the Christian belief that the dead will face Christ on the Day of Judgement, summed up in Matthew 24:27 'For as lightning cometh out of the east, and shineth even into the west; so shall also the coming of the Son of Man be.'

Satellite dishes: Tend to all face the same way as they're pointing at the same satellite. In the UK, they're normally oriented south–south-east.

Escape!

Armed with the techniques and tips outlined above, you should now be able to effectively orient yourself in the landscape, head to where you're meant to be going, lead your would-be captors a merry dance during which you outwit them completely, and melt away into the landscape.

You've done it. You've escaped from Dartmoor, and found your way to civilisation. You can now hide in the shadowy recesses of some dusty boozer and treat yourself to a victory pint – you've earned it.

The next step is to find someone to forge you the necessary papers to re-integrate yourself seamlessly back into society until the heat's off.

Sadly, you're on your own with that one.

Also worth knowing – judging distance by sight

If – heaven forbid – you do catch sight of your pursuer, it's worth knowing how far away they are. The following handy chart will help you to judge distances on sight.

Object(s) you can see	Distance at which object(s) become visible
A church steeple	9 miles
Large houses, towers, etc	6 miles
Large details on houses – chimneys and windows, etc	2.5 miles
Trunks of larger trees	1 mile
Human being (no detail – looks like a peg or post)	800 yards
Human being (colours of clothes can be distinguished)	500 yards
Human being (face can be seen)	300 yards
Human being (details of clothing can be seen – uniform details, pockets, amusing knitted motifs on sweaters, etc.)	200 yards
Human being (eyes appear as dots)	100 yards
Human being (features can be distinguished and person can be recognised)	50 yards
Human being (close enough to smell their breath)

You have spent too long consulting this chart, and are now being captured. | 0 yards |

Further tips for dealing with adverse conditions

BOGS
If you do get stuck in a deep bog, stay calm. If you panic, you'll thrash about, facilitating your descent. Use a slow breast-stroke motion to flatten your body out and 'swim' to firmer ground. If the area you're traversing is especially treacherous and boggy, you might even want to carry a large sturdy tree branch, ideally about as tall as you are. If the unthinkable happens and you do start to get sucked under, lie the branch flat and ease your back over it, in a sort of slow-motion Fosbury Flop. This may take a while but once achieved, you will stop sinking. Slowly work on freeing your legs and then carefully paddle/breast-stroke to firm ground.

RIVERS
Never enter a river unless you're sure it's the only option you have left. Rivers are dangerous and unpredictable. Never, ever enter a freezing river, as ice-cold water can kill you very quickly, and once you're in, the clock's ticking. You might also have the misfortune to be swept away under a part of the river which is still iced over, meaning you might drown. Wading is preferable to swimming, but in both cases beware of branches on the river bed which could snare you. Swimming across a river is inadvisable and should only ever be considered as a last resort in dire circumstances.

NIGHTFALL
Traversing unknown terrain at night is more difficult than doing it in the daylight, for obvious reasons, and your progress will be slower. However, it is possible, and in some cases you may have no choice. Take heart though – it's never completely dark outside, and after a time, you will be able to see. It usually takes about 30–40 minutes for the eyes to properly adjust to darkness, so you might want to wait until you can see reasonably well before setting off. Subsequent exposure to bright light (such as car headlamps) will effectively destroy your night-vision for a short while, so avoid roads and human settlements. At night, the edges of objects are more visible than the objects themselves, so try not to look directly at things if you want to see where they are.

No matter how good you are at seeing in the dark and walking about in it, any night-time walking will involve some stumbling around. You're more likely to leave tracks, and won't be able to see them, and there certainly won't be much opportunity for backwards walking-type shenanigans. It's not a good idea to traverse bogland, marsh or swamp at night. Wherever you are, walk slowly and test the ground with each step. Turning your ankle is annoying in everyday life, but during your prison break it may make the difference between capture and escape.

JAMES MAY

Crazy Golf

HOME IMPROVEMENT

Golf, as someone once observed, is a good walk spoiled, and that's a sentiment we can fervently echo in the Man Lab. Golf is, by and large, less fun than it's made out to be. To do it properly you need hundreds of acres of well-kept lawn, hundreds of pounds worth of equipment and some seriously horrible trousers.

That said, there is one manifestation of golf we can wholeheartedly endorse, and that's Crazy Golf. It's like real golf, but with all the seriousness taken out and replaced with anarchic fun. Plus, you don't have to wear a lemon-yellow Pringle sweater in order to play it (although you can if you want to – Crazy Golf imposes few rules).

Trouble is, there simply aren't enough Crazy Golf courses in the world for our liking – something you can easily help to put right by building your own Crazy Golf course at home.

Building your own Crazy Golf hole (or holes) in your own home

The beauty of this project is that you can build the hole indoors or out – whichever works best for you. If you have a backyard or garden that you feel is criminally underused, then a few miniature golf holes might just fill the gap, and add value both to your leisure hours and the market price of your house (probably).

Indoors, you'll more than likely only have space for one or possibly two holes, unless you have a spare ballroom you never use.

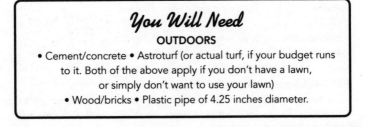

You Will Need
OUTDOORS
• Cement/concrete • Astroturf (or actual turf, if your budget runs to it. Both of the above apply if you don't have a lawn, or simply don't want to use your lawn)
• Wood/bricks • Plastic pipe of 4.25 inches diameter.

> ### INDOORS
> • Astroturf, or synthetic putting-green matting (a trip to the golf shop beckons) • Wood/bricks • Indoor putting holes or baskets.

In addition to these, you may need paint, and possibly other materials, depending on how creative you want to be. We'll get to that in a bit.

Designing the hole

The traditional Crazy Golf hole consists of a tee, a putting lane and some kind of obstacle or other twist between you and the hole. And then the hole.

The obstacle is the key feature of Crazy Golf and is where you will exercise your creativity. On real Crazy Golf courses, the obstacles vary from quite tame and relatively un-crazy obstacles, such as a slope or a dog-legged putting avenue, to really impressive and eccentric features like windmills, castles or giant heads and faces.

The design stage is key, as it will determine how playable your Crazy Golf course is. Too easy, and you'll quickly grow bored of it. Too hard and you'll also get bored of it, but for different reasons. It must be challenging but not impossible.

It must also be unique. You're designing this golftastic monstrosity, and as such you should attempt to put your individual stamp on it. After the basic rules of playability have been put in place, your Crazy Golf course can be as crazy as you can make it. What's the weirdest, most outlandish thing you can create? How will you achieve it?

If space is a premium, you can maximise what space you have by running holes side-by-side.

> **TIP:** A well-designed Crazy Golf hole should help you improve your putting, just in case you decide to take up deeply un-crazy regular golf.

> **TIP:** One good rule of thumb to bear in mind when laying out your Crazy Golf hole is that a hole in one should theoretically be possible but difficult to achieve. You might also want to award your hole a 'par'. All of this will greatly add to your hole's playability.

Building your course

Measure and lay out your hole(s) either indoors or outdoors, and begin to build. Your hole should be at least three feet wide, with wider areas at both ends for the tee and hole.

JAMES MAY

OUTDOOR COURSE

If you're doing this outdoors, you can simply lay turf to create your hole. Or, even more simply, just partition off a part of your lawn, if you have one. You can even explore the cement option, if you're happy to make your Crazy Golf holes a permanent feature.

Make holes by sinking a length of plastic pipe about six to eight inches deep. (Make sure the hole, and the plastic pipe you use to create it, are exactly 4.25 inches in diameter, in accordance with the rules of golf laid down in 1891 by the Royal and Ancient Golf Club of St Andrews.)

Sinking holes is easy to do if you're using an actual lawn or pouring your own concrete putting lane, but indoor holes may require a little more thought.

> **TIP:** Outdoor holes need about an inch of gravel at the bottom to drain rainwater. Make sure the pipe edge doesn't protrude above the grass. Check the hole regularly to make sure it doesn't clog with leaves, debris, a wayward frog, funnel-web spiders, etc.

INDOOR COURSE

If you're doing this indoors you can use indoor putting matting, available from golf shops and specially designed with the indoor game in mind. How you build your course will be determined by how long you want it to stay around.

When it comes to giving your indoor putting green a hole, there are three solutions:
1. Buy a putting basket or cup that lies on its side on the floor, or a raised hole that you putt up a slope into.
2. Drill an actual hole into the actual floor of your actual house, and fit a putting cup into it.
3. Build a sturdy raised frame, which rises six inches from the floor, and build your entire putting course on top of that.

All things considered, I'd go with option 1. But the choice is yours. For both types of course, rough out the edges of the course using lengths of 2 by 4, bricks or breeze blocks, which you can cement into place or not, depending again on how permanent you want your golf hole to be.

Make sure that the parts of your course that are meant to be flat actually are flat, so that the ball runs smoothly across them. There's a limit to how 'crazy' we want things to get.

Simple obstacles

Forget the miniature colosseum with tiny gladiators and the rotating windmill that lights up when a shot goes into the hole – we can deal with those later, when we get really creative (or indeed, not at all, when we can't be bothered). For the moment, all we need to know are the basics.

The simplest Crazy Golf obstacles are:

WEIRD-SHAPED COURSE (TWO DIMENSIONS)

- L-shaped or dog-legged putting green (making a hole-in-one very difficult – but, crucially, not impossible)
- Zig-zag (though think about how many ricochets you will need to achieve a hole-in-one)
- Spiral (a hole-in-one won't really be possible with this)

WEIRD-SHAPED COURSE (THREE DIMENSIONS)

- Raised hole (like the crater of a tiny volcano, which of course, due to the magic of Crazy Golf, it can explicitly resemble)
- Wavy depressions and hills
- Bridges to holes (meaning only an exceedingly straight putt will cut the mustard)
- Ramps (usually meaning the ball actually leaves the ground to find another part of the course)
- Obstacles on the green – Concrete shapes or even just bricks that prevent a clear shot to the hole
- Blind chutes and pocket traps, that lead nowhere

> **TIP:** If you want to make the holes as impressive as possible, you could even wire them up with lights and moving parts, although this isn't practical outside. Just remember – the more moving parts a thing has, the more liable it is to break, and the longer it will take to make.

Putt your money where your mouth is

There will be many variations on all of the above holes that you will come up with, using just a tiny bit of imagination. Remember, this project can take as much or as little effort as you are prepared to give it. If you have an open outdoor space, a large quantity of bricks and wood to rough the course out and a few lengths of pipe for holes, you could probably make an adequate course in under twenty minutes. Or you could really go to town on it. The choice is yours.

Don't lose sight of the founding principle of Crazy Golf, however – it's meant to be fun, a bit of a laugh for you and your mates. If you start worrying about gloves and clubs and groundsmanship, you might as well go and play real golf.

And nobody wants that.

Repair Shop

open

Replacing a Pane of Glass

As children, all that time spent reading the exploits of Dennis the Menace meant we all grew up very familiar with how to break a window. Kicking a football at it was probably the best-known and most frequently deployed method, with throwing a cricket bat through it and firing a pebble from a catapult at it coming in at joint second.

But now we are men, and we have put away childish things. Our window-breaking days are almost certainly behind us. It's high time we saw the other side of the issue, and learned how to replace a pane of glass.

The following instructions are for replacing a pane of glass in an ordinary wooden sash window. If you've got UPVC or metal windows, you will probably have to call in a professional.

You Will Need

• Putty • Putty knife • Hammer and chisel (not one of your best chisels, though still sharp) • Hacking knife • Sprigs (headless nails designed solely for keeping glass panels in wooden window frames, and sitting below the putty line) • A free afternoon

Before you start

Measure up for the pane of replacement glass. If it's a single glazed pane (as it's most likely to be in a wooden sash), then any glazier will be able to cut it for you. If it's a double-glazed unit, your glazier should still be able to make you a replacement, but it will take longer. You could even buy a pane of glass the approximate size, and cut it to size yourself using a glass cutter, if you're really gung-ho about this.

The rebate (the part of the sash window frame in which the pane of glass sits) is on the exterior side of the window, so that's where you'll be working. (If it's an upper-floor window, you'll probably have to do the following job up a ladder.)

Measuring up for the pane is obviously easier once all the old glass and putty have been removed (see next page) but then you have a large hole in your window while you wait for the glazier to cut the glass, which will be a magnet for burglars, pigeons, etc. If you do decide to remove the old glass and putty first, measure and cut a piece of plywood to plug the hole and secure it with screws driven into the rebate. The plywood can be removed and discarded when you fit the proper replacement glass. Being inside the rebate, the screw-holes you've made for the plywood will be buried in putty.

TIP: Before you begin, put a dust sheet down to catch all the fragments of glass, paint and old putty this operation will inevitably generate. Unless you're the Marquis de Sade, you probably don't want razor sharp chips of glass in your garden.

TIP: Be careful when you measure up for your pane as the wooden sash may well have warped in its years of service, meaning that the pane might not fit exactly. Cut out any raised parts that prevent the pane sitting flat against the frame. You should also subtract a couple of millimetres from your measurements so that the pane fits more easily into the rebate.

Replacing a broken window pane

1. Wearing thick gloves, carefully remove the shattered pane (or bits of it). Remove the old putty, leaving the rebate clear. The putty will either be so weatherbeaten that it's crumbly and friable and will come off easily, or will have hardened and almost become part of the rebate, meaning that you're going to have to hack away at it with a chisel or a hacking knife.

You may well want to wear safety glasses or goggles for this, as old putty is superb at leaping off the window frame and into your eyes in tiny fragments, which is especially annoying and dangerous if you're up a ladder.

> **TIP:** If the broken window pane is large and looks like it might collapse dangerously if dismantled, put strips of gaffa tape across it, horizontally and vertically, so the larger shards won't fall.

2. Once the rebate is clear, sand down any rough surfaces and fill any holes or cracks with wood filler. Then, paint the rebate with wood primer. This will stop the oil from the putty seeping into the grain of the wood, causing the putty to dry out too quickly and crack.

3. Once the primer has dried, press a small rope of putty all the way round the rebate, so that it covers the rebate in a very thin layer.

> **TIP:** Use the right putty. Linseed oil putty is the best for wooden-framed windows.

4. Place your new pane into the rebate and carefully press around the edges so that it beds uniformly onto the putty. Don't press down too hard – this is the point where you're most likely to break the pane. Once the pane is safely in, trim off any excess putty with a putty knife.

5. Then, tap in the sprigs so that they hold the window pane in. Putting the sprigs in should pose no risk of breaking the glass, as the side of the hammer head will rest against the glass as you gently tap them into place. One sprig every 6–10 centimetres should be enough to secure the pane in place.

6. Make a long sausage of putty and press into the edges of the glass and the rebate, covering the sprig heads and coming up to the top

Quick Tip

Getting Stuck Items Out of a Vending Machine ☑

We've all been there. You're having a bad day, and so in order to raise your spirits, you decide to buy yourself some treat or other from the vending machine . . . only to watch in horror as it gets stuck on the rotating wire coil and stays there, making it seem as if the whole universe is against you.

Well fortunately, the tips in this book are about things that actually matter, rather than hypothetical advice about fighting gorillas. Thus, we proudly present the Man Lab guide to Getting Stuck Items Out of a Vending Machine, or 'Chocs Away'.

If this happens to you, you have six options for dealing with the situation:

Bash the machine

The classic approach. Mind how you go though – best not to bang on the glass at the front, as this is quite thin and may break (which means you can take as many Yorkie bars as you want, but you will be going to A&E). Bang the sides. They're metal. They can take it.

Shake the machine

Not recommended. Vending machines are solidly built to discourage theft, and many have a weird, top-heavy centre of gravity. This means that the machine might pitch forward, crushing you. Some poor sods have actually met their end in this fashion, which is both tragic and extraordinarily undignified. So let's remove that one as a realistic option.

Buy another of the same chocolate bar

In the hope, of course, that this will dislodge both your original purchase and the new one. This approach has a few flaws however: you may have only had enough change to buy your original choc bar; you may have to leave the vending machine in order to get change (leaving your original purchase hanging temptingly in front of anyone who might then have the same idea as you); and – most horrific of all, after all of the rigmarole of getting change – your second purchase might also get stuck, leaving you in no doubt that the universe definitely has it in for you.

Good luck with this one.

Vigorously open and close the metal vending flap

The idea here is that this will create enough air movement inside to dislodge the rebellious confectionery. It's a desperate, last-ditch strategy, but it can yield results and is always worth a go, provided no one else is around. Otherwise you'll just look mental.

Contact the maintenance staff

If you're in an office or a canteen, there will be maintenance staff around, and anyone who's dealt with one of these machines for longer than forty-five minutes will sympathise with your problem. As often as not, they'll have keys and will be able to simply open the front of the machine and do what gravity failed to – i.e. give you your choc bar.

(This approach has the same flaw as running off to get change – while you're away trying to locate the bloke with the keys, someone else might have better luck dislodging your snack than you did.)

Write a stern letter to the vending-machine people

Life really is too short to do this, which is why we've prepared the following – an all-purpose, cut-out-and-keep letter of complaint to the vending-machine company. Keep a photocopy of this on your person and when you fail to get served, just send it to the manufacturer's address (which should be printed on the machine somewhere).

Together, we can do this. It's time the little guy took on the big vending conglomerates.

Best of luck.

YOUR NAME, YOUR ADDRESS

Dear Sir/Madam,
On (insert date) I attempted to buy a (insert name of chocolate bar/crisp flavour) from one of your sodding vending machines. I paid the correct money, but the (insert name of etc etc) did not drop into the vending tray, leaving me unsatisfied, saddened and blinded by an all-consuming hatred for your institution.
I am hereby writing to a) register a complaint and b) seek financial restitution.
To this end, please send (name of item again) – or the equivalent cash value – to the above address.
I greatly appreciate your co-operation in this matter.

Yours etc.,
XXXXX

the saw

Alongside the hammer, the saw is the most important item in any serious DIY-er's toolkit. And, very much like the hammer, the saw is a tool that most men feel they instinctively know all about, as if the necessary DIY know-how is somehow already implanted in their DNA. Hogwash, say I. Sawing is a vital skill, but one that you'll only acquire with practice.

Saw basics

The saw's origins are not clear – it appears to be a device developed independently by many people at many different times and places. Primitive Bronze Age saws do exist, and show surprisingly few differences from the saws of today. We know that the Ancient Egyptians also used saws, as there are illustrations of them doing just that. There's a lot of evidence that they were in use in many other places in the ancient world too – the tell-tale cut of a saw is very easy to identify.

Despite the many shapes and sizes saws come in, there are only two ways in which they cut wood – either across the grain (cross-cutting) or with the grain (ripping). The teeth of cross-cutting saws are bevelled, meaning the teeth behave as tiny cutting edges. The teeth of ripping saws are square, with a flat base, meaning that the teeth behave almost like tiny chisels, shaving off small amounts of wood as they go.

Saws you need

There are many, many different types of saw. Fortunately, the average DIY-er will only need a small selection.

A hand saw or panel saw (1): This is the saw everyone immediately thinks of when someone says 'saw' – the common or garden wood saw. Before the advent of power tools, they were the main device used for cutting all types of wood. There are actually two main types of hand

saw, with different teeth for either cross-cutting or ripping. In order to be properly prepared, get both.

A tenon saw or back saw (2): A stiff-backed saw with smaller teeth, for fine work, such as cutting joints. The back is the top of the saw blade and is usually a shiny, sturdy brass edge running along the top. To get the best results, use in conjunction with a bench-hook or a mitre box, both of which will help to get a straight cut.

Hack saw (3): A sturdy metal saw with a sturdy metal blade for cutting through sturdy metal. Also worth getting a junior hacksaw (a smaller wire-frame version of the hacksaw) for smaller jobs.

Hand-held circular saw (4): A power saw that greatly reduces the amount of time it takes to do jobs. It can cut much faster and much more accurately than a conventional hand saw. But it also makes bigger mistakes more quickly.

A jig saw (5): An extremely versatile power saw, capable of cutting curves and reasonably complex shapes.

> **TIP:** Always buy loads of replacement blades so you don't run out halfway through an important job. This applies particularly to jig saws and hacksaws.

> **TIP:** As with most tools, it's worth investing in good ones. Most DIY chains do cheap handsaws with brightly coloured plastic handles, and their worthiness and efficiency as tools can best be judged by how often you see them sticking out of skips. In addition to not lasting long, cheap saws tend to cut poorly too. You have been warned.

Saw prep

For both hand sawing and power sawing, make sure your blade is sharp and clean, and free of obstructions or sawdust.

Make sure you've marked, with a pencil and a straight edge, where you're going to cut.

Make sure your work is secured and won't move while you cut it. With a hand saw, this will be annoying. With a power saw, this could lead to amputation.

> **TIP:** Some chipboards contain flecks of metal, which will ruin saw blades. Cut this stuff using something with a replaceable blade, such as the jig saw. Better still, don't use chipboard. It's not proper.

Using the saw

Hand saw: Get into a comfortable cutting position, one that won't strain your back. With the first cut, drag the saw towards you, making a neat groove. Then you can start to saw in earnest. Guide the saw gently and let it find its own pace, rather than forcing down onto it. Pay extra attention to the first few strokes, as they will dictate where the cut goes. If you do this badly, you'll be 'fighting' the saw to stick to your cut line for the rest of the cut.

Cut on the waste side of your pencil line. Take your time and be as neat as possible.

Power saw: Make sure the saw runs cleanly along any pencil lines you've made, using a clamped-down straight edge to guide you if need be.

> **TIP:** If you're cutting old wood with a power saw, beware of any old nails or other metal fixings which may lie embedded in the timber. They can blunt the blade, and cause the saw to jump (the same goes for any large knots).

> **TIP:** Comfort is the key to accurate sawing. Make sure you're in a comfortable standing position, and try to think of the saw as an extension to the movements of your arm. An accurate, comfortable cut means the saw will behave. An inaccurate, laboured cut means that the saw will resist you, and make complaining noises in the wood.

> **TIP:** Use a Workmate or workbench to cut on. Do not use a wobbly chair. (Interestingly, the Workmate was invented by a chap called Ron Hickman, who was inspired to create it after getting sick of using a wobbly chair to saw stuff on. Even more interestingly, Hickman also designed the original Lotus Elan.)

Saw safety

All saws are dangerous if used incorrectly. All saws should be treated with care and respect.

We've covered the basics as we went along, but it can't hurt to repeat them: secure your work and make sure your fingers are nowhere near the blade.

If cutting with a power saw, always make sure the power cable is nowhere near the blade and use ear defenders.

Where possible, give yourself plenty of space to work in.

Other handy saws

JAPANESE SAW

An odd-looking saw consisting of a very thin blade mounted to the top of a long handle. Unlike its European counterparts, the Japanese saw cuts on the pull stroke rather than the push. These saws are very handy for general joinery work, and can cut in places that larger and more cumbersome saws can't and are capable of producing extremely fine cuts of just ½ mm thickness.

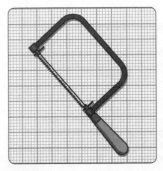

COPING SAW

A metal-framed saw with an ultra-thin blade of only a couple of millimetres' thickness, the coping saw is designed to cut complex shapes as the blade can change direction very quickly. The blade is given extra strength by being held in tension, but this doesn't stop the blades from snapping fairly often.

MAN LAB MANUAL

FLOORBOARD SAW

A strange-looking tool in which the teeth continue to run around the nose of the saw, which is either rounded or semicircular. This odd arrangement is designed to cut through floorboards *in situ*, meaning that the saw excels at this job but isn't recommended as your first choice for other tasks.

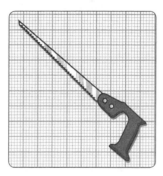

KEYHOLE SAW

A long, narrow-bladed sword-like saw, designed to cut from a start as simple as a drilled hole. Also reasonably good at cutting complex shapes, though the teeth of this saw are quite large and the blade is usually thick, meaning that precision is not achievable. Really complex shapes are best done with the coping saw.

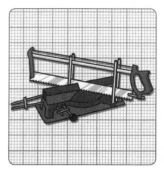

MITRE SAW

If you need to cut wood to a precise angle, you'll almost certainly have to invest in one of these. Perfect for cutting architrave, beading and other wood details to an exact spec, the mitre saw is available in either old-fashioned manual or newfangled automated variations. Opinion is split among woodworkers as to which is better – you'll have to make up your own mind.

Indoor Garden

'He who plants a garden, plants happiness' goes one Chinese proverb. 'If you want to be happy for a lifetime, plant a garden' goes another. Yet another says 'he who leads a life of plants, plants life' – except we made that one up.

Nonetheless, the message is clear. Gardens – and the feeling of satisfaction derived from creating and maintaining them – go an enormous way to contributing to our psychological wellbeing.

The only trouble is that these days, what with most of us living in crowded cities rather than the countryside, the reality of having a garden of your own is getting harder and harder to achieve. Conventional wisdom says that most of us will have to do without.

We disagree. How is man's soul meant to flourish without a garden? How can he commune with his beloved nature if a garden is denied him? Where else can he retire when troubled with an especially bad bout of wind?

The Man Lab Indoor Garden

Your fully realised Man Lab will already be, in many ways, a paradise. It will have a well-stocked bar, a rest and relaxation area with two sofas in it that hardly smell at all, and its own railway. Indeed, when you rest from your labours of creating it, and look upon it, lo, you will see that it is good – but you will also see that it can be better. It lacks a certain something – a connection with nature. It has no obvious spots of outstanding natural beauty.

With this in mind, let's set about constructing our own indoor garden. A garden that will be the rival of any of its swankier outdoor cousins. A tranquil place that will inspire us to greater heights of achievement through its effortless green majesty. Or at the very least, furnish us with some lettuce.

Indoor Gardening – the pros

An indoor garden environment is (in theory) an almost completely controllable environment, and that makes it one of the most efficient gardens you can grow. Here are some other reasons you should seriously consider an indoor garden.

- **It'll be less hassle.** We're not saying here that there will be NO watering or hard work. But those hardships will be greatly reduced in an indoor garden, as opposed to an outdoor one. You also shouldn't have to weed it.
- **You can grow stuff all year round** (and it'll be better stuff too). As your environment is an artificial one, there are no seasons, and you will control the light and temperature, like a god. Also, studies have shown that fruits and vegetables grown in an indoor hydroponic garden taste better than outdoor-grown produce – and they also contain more vitamins.
- **It will enhance your quality of life.** As well as being aesthetically appealing, an indoor garden will help to detox your house (or your Man Lab) by processing some of the pollutants and dispelling some of the persistent 'boy smell' that permeates any environment inhabited by more than no men.

Another advantage of your indoor garden is that it can be any shape or size you like – most indoor gardening equipment is designed with flexibility in mind. You can maximise your growing potential even in the most weirdly shaped space.

(In case you were wondering, 'hydroponic' simply means 'soilless', and stuff in a hydroponic garden is grown in a nutrient solution. Our garden won't be soilless, but a hydroponic garden might be something you want to consider if you're really serious about this, and you're a huge fan of highly vitaminised vegetables.)

You Will Need

- Special indoor growing lights (see below for more on this)
- Seed-starting trays (get the ones with the transparent plastic lids)
- Plant pots of various sizes • Potting compost
- Gravel • Seeds/cuttings/plants

More than likely there's tons more equipment you'll find yourself needing as soon as you begin, but these are the absolute necessities.

Setting up your garden – the basics

Although so far we appear to be advocating the gung-ho, gonzo spirit of gardening, laced with a DIY punk aesthetic, it is nonetheless worth setting some time aside before you start to consider the best place to grow your own indoor garden.

Some basic rules to observe:

- Even a location as small as your house/flat will have its own extremes of temperature, which should be avoided. So a poorly insulated, draughty extension is out, as is anywhere with a lot of dry heat. Find somewhere with an even, stable temperature.
- South-facing is best. In the northern hemisphere, a south-facing room gets the most in the way of natural sunlight, thus helping your plants and cutting down on your electricity bills. Be careful, though, as most indoor plants can't tolerate direct sunlight – a net curtain should be placed over the window to diffuse the light.
- Give thought to where you place plants in your garden. Find out which plants need the most light, and which prefer more shade, and plant accordingly. It's worth getting this right at the very start, as moving growing plants around is far more of a faff than moving seeds and seed trays around. Also, label your plants after planting, as it's very easy to forget what's growing where when all you can see are trays full of soil.
- Your plants may still need to be moved if they grow tall and thin and pale by growing too fast towards the light. The technical term for this is 'etiolated'.

What to grow?

There are limits to what you can grow in an indoor garden – mangrove trees and sequoias are out, for example – but a huge variety of fun, interesting, useful and, above all, edible plants are capable of being grown indoors (as well as quite a few smokeable varieties, but we shan't dwell on that). So choose wisely and well. Here are some suggestions:

VEGETABLES

The best kinds of vegetables to grow indoors are ones that take up very little space, like leaf lettuce. Other vegetables that can be grown indoors, but take up more space, are things like tomatoes, aubergines, peppers and cucumbers. Herb gardens can also work well for very small spaces.

Some crops do very poorly indoors, so be aware of which crops won't work. Corn, squashes and most brassicas (cabbages and broccoli) aren't worth planting indoors as they tend to fare very badly in an indoor environment.

Vegetables that do well indoors include peppers, chard, spinach, lettuce, leeks, carrots, celeriac, radishes, peas, French beans, tomatoes and aubergine.

> **TIP:** Most vegetables need about six hours of direct light every day and temperatures between 65 and 95 degrees Fahrenheit. They also need a great intensity of light.

> **TIP:** Water your vegetables with 2 inches of water a week, which is approximately how much they'd get outdoors. If you're running a heater to keep temperatures high enough for the plants, monitor the soil moisture and water the plants more often if the soil is drying out too quickly.

FLOWERS

As the indoor environment is so eminently controllable, you can grow many strange and exotic flowers indoors, provided you're willing to put the work in. Flowers and succulents clean and freshen the air, provide oxygen and humidify the room.

TOP 5 FLOWERS TO GROW INDOORS:
Orchids

Orchids are regarded by many as the most beautiful and appealing of all flowers. There are about 100,000 different hybrids of orchid in the world, but only a few are suitable to be grown by blokes in the comfort of their own living room. They're a slight pain in the backside to feed, water and maintain, and they are fussy about temperature, but the flowers more than make up for all that.

Despite their glamorous appearance, orchids have a less than glamorous name, deriving as it does from the Greek for 'testicle'.

Bromeliads

Rainforest plants that flower in a spectacular array of colours. Although they can take several years to come to flower, the flowers are beautiful and last for several months when they do arrive. Despite the fact that they look rather high maintenance, Bromeliads are relatively easy to care for. They're happy at room temperature, needing higher temperatures only to flower. They hardly ever need repotting, and you water them by simply filling the rosette in the centre.

Peace lily

Alternatively known by the far-less-snappy formal name of *Spathiphyllum wallisii*, the peace lily is a favourite indoor flower, producing large, sail-like white blooms, reminiscent of proper lilies, every autumn.

Poinsettia

'Well, I wish it could be Christmas, every day . . .' sang Roy Wood of Wizzard. And you can convince yourself that's the case for at least six months of the year by keeping this festive favourite in bloom long after Twelfth Night. Though it does flower, the joy of a poinsettia is its crimson foliage rather than the rather rubbish yellow flowers it produces. You'll normally have to bin it after it's flowered, but take cuttings and you should have a deep red Christmas every year.

Jasmine

A fragrant houseplant is a real joy, especially somewhere like the Man Lab, which will largely smell of burning and socks. Jasmine has a pleasant, heady aroma and can be grown fairly easily indoors. Remember to keep the plant cool in winter and put it outdoors during summer. It also likes plenty of light and water. Jasmine's a very fast climber, however, so you'll have to prune it regularly. Make sure you get a fragrant variety, as non-smelly jasmines do exist.

CACTI

Cacti continue to be very poorly understood by the general public, who seem to have many of them in their homes without ever really understanding what they are, what they do or why they bought them in the first place. Hence a lot of cacti indoors are in a sorry state, covered in dust and consigned to a part of the house seldom visited.

This is completely unfair – cacti are hardly dynamic but if cared for properly they can be fascinating and rewarding to grow.

They're a no-no if you have pets, however.

OTHER HOUSE PLANTS

The full catalogue of plants you can grow in your indoor man-garden, just for the joy of growing them, is huge and wide-ranging, and would take up many volumes. Suffice it to say that, like many of the life-improving projects in this book, you can become as involved and creative in this as you wish, and, if you're prepared to put the work in, you'll be amazed at what you can grow.

Planting

So – you've got all your stuff from the garden centre. You've identified the most suitable part of your flat/house/Man Lab in which to place your garden. You've chosen your plants. It's time to build and sow your garden. Like so:
1. Fill the seed trays with good-quality seed compost or multi-purpose compost (it will say on the bag if you can use it for both seeds and plants). Press the compost down lightly, water thoroughly with tap water, then plant your seeds.
2. Lower your adjustable light source to about 3 inches above the seed trays.
3. Wait for the plants to sprout. This can take anything from three days to three weeks.
4. Remove the plastic dome lids from the seed trays when the new plants are pushing against them.
5. Once the plants have grown a few inches, their roots will probably have outgrown the seed tray. It's time to repot them in larger pots. Use pots a size larger than the seed tray compartments, with holes drilled for drainage at the bottom. Fill with fresh multi-purpose compost or a compost that says it's for seedlings – they need more nutrients at this stage. Then, put the plant with its root-and-soil base in the pot, and carefully pour soil around the edges, patting down until the pot is level. Water well.

And that's it. You're now an indoor gardener.

Lights

As technological development is dragging its heels yet again, you can't have an actual tiny sun in your flat yet, and an indoor garden won't work with ordinary household bulbs, so you're going to have to get some lights. Although getting the right lights for your indoor garden is crucial, the specifics of which hardware you need is actually quite boring. Nevertheless, do not be tempted to skip this bit. If you buy the wrong lights, you'll regret it in the long run.

Briefly then . . . there are three main types of grow lights: Incandescent, fluorescent and high-intensity discharge (HID). We can discount incandescent lights straight off for our purposes as they aren't very efficient and have a limited light spectrum. So that leaves us with fluorescent and HID.

Fluorescent lights: Inexpensive to run as they don't use that much electricity. They also don't generate much heat, so can be placed close to the plants without harming them. Fluorescent bulbs also cost much less than HID bulbs, and tend to be smaller and more compact, but don't produce as much light, however. As the light produced is not high intensity, fluorescent lamps tend to work better with plants that thrive in mid- to low-light intensity.

High-intensity discharge lights: Although they're more efficient and produce more light than fluorescents, they also produce more heat, are more expensive, and will require the additional maintenance and expense of a ballast (a device that regulates the current). They also take a long time to warm up – in some cases, up to 100 hours of burning time before the light intensity stabilises. There are also two types of HI lighting – metal halide, which produces light in the blue spectrum, and sodium, which produces light in the red and yellow spectrum. For best results, you'll probably need some of both.

To make your indoor gardening system more efficient, you should consider using reflectors and light movers. Also, don't forget that many types of grow-lighting require a ballast to ignite the bulb, pushing costs up further.

Remember – which light is best for you and your crops very much depends on what you're growing. Give this some thought before you purchase.

> TIP: A general rule for your garden's required lighting: 1000W will adequately penetrate about 16–25 square feet of plant area.

> TIP: Light intensity decreases significantly the further away from the light your plants are. Make sure they're close to your plants.

Indoor garden pests

So far, we've made the indoor gardening experience seem like a fairly easy and comfortable one, but there are several different threats which might blight your new-found Eden. Your significant other might get sick of the attention you lavish on it, and bin it in a fit of pique. The thermostat might fail and destroy your hard work overnight. The dog might trample it. Or – much more likely – it will fall foul of a swarm of pests.

Here are some of the most common household pests to look out for:

APHIDS
Green or black insects that can become very numerous very quickly, and threaten the life of the plant. They like sap, so are a special menace to younger plants.

Look out for: Sticky patches or leaves on the plant. This is honeydew, which the aphids secrete when they gorge on sap. Look out also for grey or white specks on the plant – these are cast-off aphid casings. Ew.

SPIDER MITES
Tiny brick-red mites that congregate on the underside of leaves. Hard to spot until they're established, and very hard to get rid of.

Look out for: Speckling or silvering on leaves; leaves falling off.

FUNGUS GNATS
Small black flies (adults); tiny maggots in soil (larvae).

Look out for: A lot of movement when the pot is disturbed, which then settles down. Tiny flies and maggots in the compost.

WHITE FLY
White, moth-like flies.

Look out for: Young flies and eggs under the leaves. Colonies of adults which fly up and re-settle when the plant is disturbed.

THRIPS
Tiny black flies which move from leaf to leaf.

Look out for: Silver streaks on leaves, stunted plant growth and disrupted flower growth.

As well as insect pests, your plants will also be at the mercy of plant diseases such as mould, mildew and root rot. Inspect your plants carefully and often to arrest the early signs of these infections and infestations.

To get rid of all the above you can either use a chemical pesticide – although using this in the home and on food crops has obvious drawbacks – or buy a sponge impregnated with predatory nematodes (microscopic predators which will patrol your plants, eating most of the pests). There are also natural pesticides such as citric acid you can buy. Or you can pick off the bugs with your fingers and squash them. Some people find this a very rewarding and pleasurable experience.

Conclusion
These are only basic rules, but they should furnish you with enough information to establish your own indoor Shangri-La. You've beautified an entire corner of your Man Lab and, what's more, you can now grow your own lettuce.

> **TIP:** Isolate an infected plant for treatment, so the pests can't spread. If it looks really sick, get rid of it so that it doesn't infect the healthy plants.

> **TIP:** Put a timer on the lights to simulate day and night conditions, and to make sure you don't overexpose plants to light. Plants need dark as well as light to grow.

Repair Shop
open

Repairing a Bicycle Puncture

Apparently, bike shops have seen a huge rise in clueless blokes coming in and asking for help with nothing more troublesome than a puncture. So rather than announce yourself to the world as a complete cretin, simply follow this handy step-by-step guide to mending a punctured bicycle tyre.

Every cyclist will get a puncture at one time or another. If you're going to ride a bike, best familiarise yourself with how to fix one.

Here's what you will need to fix a puncture: 1 – a pump compatible with your bike's valves; 2 – tyre levers; 3 – sandpaper, patches, chalk and rubber cement; 4 – spare inner tubes; 5 – a many-slotted bicycle spanner; 6 – cheese and pickle sandwich to eat while you work.

Invert the bike and remove the punctured wheel, either by flicking the quick-release levers or, if your bike doesn't have them, removing the nuts with your spanner. Brakes should also have a quick-release lever.

> **TIP:** If it's obvious where the puncture is (you can see a nail sticking out of the tyre, say) it is possible to fix it without removing the wheel. Simply half remove the tyre, pull the inner tube out and repair it.

Using the tyre levers, lever one side of the tyre off. Most bike tyres are clincher tyres – tyres that fit into the wheel rim. They can be tough to remove, so take care not to further damage the inner tube as you remove the tyre.

Carefully remove the inner tube. You may have to unscrew a collar nut on the air valve. The puncture may be obvious at this stage, but if it isn't, fear not. Scrutinise every inch of your inner tube and locate the puncture. You may need to pump a lot of air in for the hole to be obvious. If you can't see the puncture, try inflating the tyre and listening, or feeling, for escaping air.

If the puncture still isn't obvious after all that, then it's bucket-of-water time.

Hold the inner tube underwater and gently squeeze it. A stream of bubbles should emerge from the puncture. This method is also a good way of detecting faults in the valve. (A nearby roadside café should be able to loan you a bucket of water, but you'll probably have to buy and eat a full fried breakfast to compensate them for the abuse of their hospitality.)

Once you've located the hole, rough up the area around it with sandpaper. This will clean the rubber and provide a rough surface to help your patch stick better. You'll have to dry the tube first if you submerged it in water.

Put rubber cement on the inner tube. Wait for the glue to become tacky, then place the patch firmly over the hole. Be reasonably generous with the rubber cement and spread it slightly beyond the area of the patch. Put chalk dust over the repair so that it doesn't stick to the tyre. Finish eating your fried breakfast, if applicable.

See if you can locate the sharp object that punctured your tube. Carefully run your fingers round the inside of the tyre, or run a piece of cloth round it. Once located, discard. Check for any other obstructions.

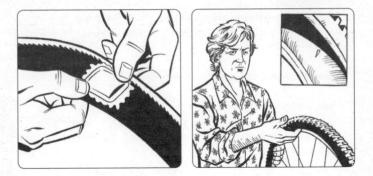

Once the glue has dried, carefully replace the inner tube, starting at the valve, then the tyre, taking care not to pinch the inner tube. Having reassembled the inner tube and tyre, pump it up a bit and then bounce it around its circumference, to make sure the tube isn't pinched.

Replace your wheel. Pump the inner tube back up. If you've done it correctly, the repair should hold. And you're done! But remember to replace the patched tube as soon as possible. The repair won't last forever.

If you've eaten both a cheese and pickle sandwich and a full English breakfast, as well as drinking three cups of tea, you might want to have a little lie-down about now.

To minimise punctures, always keep your tyres inflated to the correct pressure. Air leaks slowly out of even the best tyre valves, so always pump them up before your journey.

TIP: If you ride a bike a lot, remember to carry a pump and a patch kit, and even replacement inner tubes, at all times. Replace your cheese and pickle sandwich regularly.

Check your tyres before and after you ride for any sharp objects they might have picked up. This goes double for days when you have to cycle in the rain, as the conditions are better for making stuff stick to the tyre. Stuff that's stuck to the tyre can work its way in as you ride.

Good luck and Godspeed!

TIP: Never be tempted to ride home on a flat tyre, as it renders the bike unrideable, as you will damage your tyre and wheel rims.

tool of the week: the plane

Sadly, due to the decline of proper man-knowledge in this country, most modern blokes will only recognise the plane as something they've seen nailed to the rafters of a fake Irish pub to add 'atmosphere'. This is a sad fate for one of the most important tools ever devised – not to mention one of the most satisfying to use.

In the interests of rectifying this state of affairs, let me introduce you to the Mr Smooth of the toolbox – the humble plane.

Plane basics

Considering how long human beings have been working with wood, planes arrived somewhat late on the scene, around two thousand years ago. The earliest planes have been found at Pompeii (though there's evidence to suggest they were in use beforehand) and the basic design has changed surprisingly little over the last two thousand years. Indeed, easily recognisable woodworking planes were brought up from the wreck of the Tudor warship *Mary Rose*, a handy bit of kit for the upkeep of a wooden vessel. The modern plane as we know it was born in the nineteenth century when Leonard Bailey produced a cast-iron plane, the patent for which was bought by Stanley. (It's a testament to the quality of Bailey's design that it's still in use today.)

Planes you need

Cliché enthusiasts would no doubt tell you that there are 'a bewildering array' of planes, all designed for a different, specific purpose. Serious woodworkers place great value on planes, and usually have as many as they can find space for.

Most home DIY-ers will be using the plane for a limited number of tasks, however, so we can rule out some of the more obscure ones. The ones you'll probably end up using most are:

Jack plane: A sturdy, cast-iron plane with a good solid weight. (A good weight will make the plane easier to control.)

Small jack plane: Also known as a 'smoothing plane'. As the name suggests, this is a smaller version of the jack plane. These will suffice for most routine smoothing and chamfering jobs.

Planes are categorised by number, which refers to the length of the plane. So a jack plane is a number 6 whereas a small jack or smoothing

plane is a number 4 or 5. This numbering system is the same across all makes, so if you go into a shop and ask for a Stanley no. 6, it will be the same as a Record no. 6. Worth knowing: The smallest planes – number 1 – are very rare and can go for as much as £1,000 at auction.

> **TIP:** If you're serious about assembling a proper toolkit, you may want to look at obtaining a block plane – a smaller plane for cutting end grain and cross-grain – and a bullnose plane, which is thin and small and is capable of planing in extremely cramped areas. And many others, if you wish.

> **TIP:** It's worth spending a bit of extra cash to get reliable, good-quality planes. Cheapo planes don't last as long, and tend to be lighter, meaning that they're more likely to 'chatter' – dance and shudder on the wood – which of course defeats the object of the exercise.

Know your plane

A plane is a complex instrument and has been in use for thousands of years, in many different times and places. As a result, many of the parts are known by different names, but here's a summary of the best-known ones.

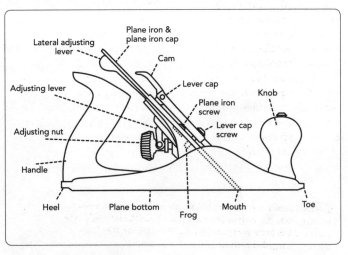

Plane preparation

Like their less sophisticated cousins the chisels, plane blades have to be sharpened regularly for the best results. The best way to do this is

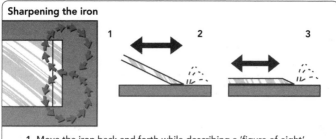

Sharpening the iron

1
2
3

1. Move the iron back and forth while describing a 'figure of eight'…
2. … all the while holding it at the correct angle.
3. Finish by stroking away the burr on the opposite side.

manually – by rubbing the blade (or iron, as it's known) on an oilstone (or a waterstone, which is less messy), until the edge is clean and keen (you can buy both types of stone from DIY shops).

Check that your blade is satisfactorily fixed and isn't projecting too far, as this can damage both wood and blade.

Don't assume before you start that a plane will work perfectly – even a brand new one will probably require 'tuning'. One of the best and easiest-to-apply improvements for your plane is to get a thicker, heavier iron for it. Most mass-market planes have thin blades as they're easier to sharpen, but they don't stand up well to the stresses and strains of planing hard woods. Fit your plane with a thicker blade and it will greatly improve its performance.

Also, don't assume that your plane's sole is perfectly flat, especially with an older plane – check it with a straight edge and a bright light, and this should reveal any bumps or raised parts. It's especially important that the area in front of the mouth is perfectly flat. Flattening the sole – or 'lapping' as it's known – is hard work, involving a special 'lapping table', silicon carbide powder, oil, water and a lot of elbow grease. You may have to consult a professional in order to lap your plane correctly, but it's worth doing if you're serious about proper planing.

When you're happy that the blade is sharp, and securely and correctly positioned, you can start planing.

> **TIP:** Remember – a plane straddles the divide between a tool (a device used to manipulate the environment) and a machine (the same, but with moving parts). Get to know your plane. Be confident you can take it apart, oil it and put it back together again in good working order.

> **TIP:** Make sure you're familiar with the lever cap and the depth-adjustment knob, so you know how to position the blade correctly and keep it there.

JAMES MAY

Using the plane

These are the basics:

- Make sure your posture is comfortable and relaxed. Put the plane to the wood.
- Push the plane smoothly and firmly along, keeping pressure on the back of the plane, especially at the end of your stroke.
- Guide the plane as carefully as possible.
- Lift the plane off the wood and back to the start for the next stroke. NEVER drag it back along the wood.

> **TIP:** Always try to plane in the direction of the grain (though there are occasional exceptions to this rule).

> **TIP:** Use a try square or a metal ruler to check the accuracy of your work.

> **TIP:** As with the chisel, always secure the wood you're going to work on before you start – with clamps or a vice. A good idea is to put odds and ends of cut-off wood between the vice/clamps and the wood you're working on, so your finished article doesn't get vice/clamp marks all over it.

Top Jobs for Planes

- Giving a professional finish to timber
- Cleaning up joints and joins in wood • Shaving doors to fit better

> **TIP:** If you're smoothing down two identical pieces of wood, and you're pushed for time, you can sometimes get away with clamping them together and planing them simultaneously.

Plane safety and storage

Planes are by and large a lot safer than chisels, but they should still be treated with respect. Common sense should tell you there's no need to touch the edge of the blade at any time.

Never store a plane on the base, or sole plate – where the blade projects. If possible, store it in a wooden box or rack where the blade isn't touching anything. When laying on the bench, put it on its side.

Get into the habit of retracting the blade on your plane a couple of turns every time you put it away.

Six lame plane puns that didn't make it into this feature:
• Plane sailing • Plane stupid
• Plane ridiculous
• Plane for all to see • High planes drifter
• No plane, no gain

Wiring a Plug ☑

Early on in the creation of Man Lab, we made a list of key tasks that the modern man seemed unable to do anymore. Remarkably, and following a brief survey of the youths in the Lab, one of these turned out to be 'wiring a plug'.

With that in mind, we present to you the Man Lab definitive guide to wiring a standard UK plug.

Basics

Your basic plug uses a standard 3-core flex, consisting of three strands of copper wire sheathed in coloured insulation.

The three wires are live, neutral and earth. They do the following jobs:

Live – Carries the current from the electricity supply to your laptop/ hairdryer/Breville sandwich toaster/whatever.

Neutral – Carries current back to the service panel, thus completing the circuit.

Earth – Normally carries no current, but is there as a safety feature. Will carry current if something goes wrong or if it's been wired incorrectly.

Needless to say: never touch any of the wires.

Colour codes

The three wires are colour-coded as follows:

Brown – Live
Blue – Neutral
Green and yellow – Earth

This has always struck me, and everyone else, as confusing. Why isn't earth brown? Why isn't live red? Shouldn't neutral be a sort of beige-y colour? And so on.

Fortunately – and this is the clever bit – you don't have to remember what all the wires do. You just have to remember where they go.

Where do they go?

The following mnemonic will help you remember where the various wires should be.

The second letter of 'brown' is R, so that goes on the right. The second letter of 'blue' is L, so that goes on the left. 'Yellow' has a double letter in the middle, same as 'middle'. So that goes in the middle.

So: B**R**own – **R**ight; B**L**ue – **L**eft; Ye**LL**ow – Mi**DD**le

Hopefully, once learned, you will never forget this.

Right then – wiring a plug

(In this case, we'll assume that you're replacing an old plug with a new one.)

• Unplug your device, and make absolutely certain there's no current running through it.

• Unscrew the casing of the old plug with a flat-head screwdriver.

• Unscrew the terminal screws keeping the old wires in place, freeing them.

• Unscrew the silver flex clamp screws, and pull the flex out of the base.

• Thread the flex into the new plug.

• Secure the flex, using the silver flex clamp screws. ALWAYS secure the flex by clamping down the outer flex, not the insulated wires within. (You can trim the wires back with wire cutters or pliers if they're too long.)

• Screw the appropriate wires into the appropriate terminals. Once again, that's brown on the right, blue on the left and yellow (and green) in the middle. Make sure the wires are securely screwed into the terminals, and there's no copper showing. The insulation of each wire should come snugly up to the terminal. While you're there, check the fuse is sound, and is the correct fuse value for the appliance. Fitting the wrong fuse means risking an electrical fire. If you're not sure what amp fuse you should use, check with the appliance manufacturer.

• Replace the casing.

Of course, nowadays, most plugs are sealed units, which means that you don't need to do any of the above. Which doesn't mean it isn't worth knowing.

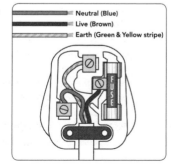

Neutral (Blue)
Live (Brown)
Earth (Green & Yellow stripe)

! *Common-sense disclaimer: Electricity is dangerous. Always make sure appliances are unplugged before you start fiddling about with them. For anything more complicated than wiring a plug, probably best to call a qualified electrician. Don't use a hairdryer in the bath, etc. etc.*

JAMES MAY

INSTALLING A
TRAIN SET
IN YOUR
WORKPLACE

In the early 1980s, the must-have toy for boys under 10 was Big Trak. Big Trak – which looked like a moon buggy might if it had been designed by a drunk Sir Clive Sinclair – was advertised as your programmable servant, an indispensable mobile butler that could be programmed to fulfil basic household tasks. Sadly, in reality, Big Trak was a jerky electronic simpleton, and the chances of him transporting a glass of Tizer across the living room without spilling it on the carpet or himself were extraordinarily low.

Although Big Trak had many faults, however, we held that the basic idea – using a toy as a handy transport system in the home – was a sound one. Maybe all that needed changing in this plan was the toy.

And so it was that we set about fitting the Man Lab with a fully-integrated man-serving railway.

Model railways – a 'hobby for the million'

Writing in *The Boys' Book of Model Railways* in 1956, Ernest F. Carter observes that model railway building is truly a 'hobby for the million' – a pastime deserving of its enormous following – as 'it offers such unlimited scope for personal individuality and ability'. He goes on to observe that the appeal of a model railway lies in the fact that it is . . . 'always complete yet never finished; and it is this queer mixture of 'collecting' and constructional work which seems to be the underlying reason for the appeal of Model Railwaying to the average handyman.'

Although the golden age of model railwaying may have peaked roughly ten minutes after Ernest F. Carter penned those words, there can be no doubt that model railways retain an enduring appeal for blokes even today.

You Will Need

If you are seriously going to build a model railway round your home/
studio/office/place of work – and we strongly recommend that
everyone at least considers it – then you'll need the following:
• Lots of sheets of plywood, for your baseboards. You
can use other materials, but whatever you decide on needs to be
tough and thick enough so that it will fully support your locomotive
and track and won't bend or flex • Lots of pine battening
• A decent quality model locomotive and trucks
• Lots and lots of track • Some more track. You almost certainly
didn't buy enough • A signalling system • Many tools, but most
essentially a jig saw to cut your baseboards.

TIP: Make sure in the hobby shop that your locomotive, trucks and track
are all a compatible gauge and are capable of freighting loads. Hobby shops
tend to be staffed by men who know everything and more about model railways,
so ask one of them.

God's wonderful railway

Your first task, having secured all the necessary equipment, is to design
your railway. This will largely be dictated by the size of the area you have
to set your network in and the locations your small-objects express will
be most use stopping at.

TIP: Think carefully before revealing to anyone important to you that you are working on a 'model railway'. Not everyone realises that toy trains are the hobby of kings and the inspiration of philosophers.

Be imaginative – there's nothing to stop your locomotive running through and behind things, and crossing large gaps, if you're prepared to put the work in. Hobby shops will sell many accessories for model railways that you can utilise in your layout – bridges and tunnels are especially helpful. Make sure you know what's available before you begin.

Pay particular attention to curves and gradients, as these will test the locomotive more than running on a straight. It's generally not good to have your track rising as it exits from the kitchen area of the Man Lab, as the trucks will probably be fully loaded, placing extra stress on your engine.

TIP: If you do put in tunnels, make sure they're high enough to accommodate tall loads, such an ambitiously high stack of Pringles.

Construction

We will assume that you're building the track to be a permanent addition to your Man Lab.

Cut your lengths of baseboard in accordance with the plans that you've made. We can further assume, for the purposes of convenience, that your railway will be at roughly tabletop (waist) height for the entirety

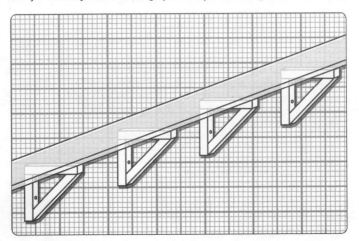

of its run. The baseboard it runs on will therefore be supported either by brackets of 45-degree pine battening, that support the track by being screwed into a wall, (see illustration) or, where a wall isn't available, by viaduct-like struts of pine battening reaching to the floor (see other illustration):

Either way, make sure that the baseboard is absolutely level all the way round and is properly supported.

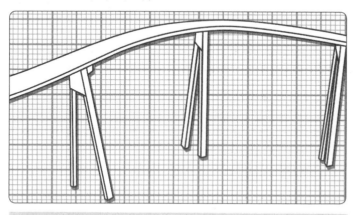

> **TIP:** Use your track as a rough template when it comes to drawing your baseboard. This is especially handy for curves and other oddly-shaped bits.

> **TIP:** If the baseboard isn't as rigid as you'd like, you can reinforce it with wooden framing underneath. This will provide rigidity and strength to your track.

> **TIP:** Make sure that any places where the path of the railway runs across the path of human beings is accessible to both – you might want to build a lifting flap that raises a section of track, allowing access.

Laying the track

Secure track to baseboard by either a strong adhesive or very fine pins sold for the purpose. Any way that works is acceptable really – even double-sided sticky tape will do. (The man who works in the hobby shop, who looks like Roger Whittaker and smells of tobacco and peppermints, will almost certainly have a strong opinion on the best way to secure track to baseboard, so ask him.)

At the end of all this, you should have a fully laid model railway track.

A NOTE ABOUT GAUGE

It's also worth considering what sort of gauge will serve your network best. The most popular model railway gauge is 00, but it's a bit small for transporting anything larger than peanuts and olives. A better bet is 0-gauge (twice as big, i.e. eight times the volume as far as a coal truck is concerned), and G-scale. The one we used for our Man Lab was 0-gauge (using Bassett-Lowke rolling stock – now part of Hornby). G-scale is for large models of narrow-gauge trains, and is useful for railways that run outdoors, or carry larger loads. Germany's LGB is the main maker. It's a very versatile system and the wagons are nice and big.

Controlling your network

This is another topic that could fill an entire book, and does in some specialist shops. The controlling mechanisms of model railways are part of the joy of having them, as they can be endlessly fiddled with and modified by the railway's owner. Many different systems exist, but they all do pretty much the same basic things.

For our purposes, however, we simply need a control which will start the train, indicate when it's been loaded, and then bring it to us. The man in the hobby shop will doubtless have some ideas where this is concerned too, but this is what we arrived at:

The Bell Signal system

In order to get the maximum from your own Man Lab railway, you might want to consider installing a modern version of what, in the glorious early days of rail, was known as a Bell Signalling system.

You Will Need

- A 'master box', at your engine's main depot (probably the kitchen, let's be honest). This is basically a signal with numbers that light up on it, corresponding to stops along the track
- Bell-pushes that activate the lights on the master box and inform the main depot which part of the network is summoning. A bell should also sound with a loud bong when they are activated. Every stop on the line gets a bell-push.

Once you've decided which stations are which, and which numbers will represent them, you need to devise instructions, and print and distribute them to each stop on your network, in the form of a handy station-master's card.

Which should look something like this:

STATION	STOP NUMBER
Kitchen	1
Bog	2
Office	3
Workshop	4
Seating area	5

BONGS	ACTION
One bong	Send train/ continue
Two bongs	Reverse train
Bong when running	Stop

That way, the person controlling the train in the kitchen knows when to stop the train, and the person in the place the train is going to knows to bong once to get the train to stop. What's more, they know to bong twice to get the train to reverse, now carrying their Post-it note request for a bag of peanuts, or whatever.

NOTE: (make sure the train is well-stocked with Post-it notes).

This bong-based signalling system seems to work very well – but it does rely on people in the other parts of the Man Lab being generous enough to take a couple of minutes to fulfil your request.

Whooo whooo

And there it is. You have rigged out your manspace with its own bespoke railway system. And, unlike most of the rail networks of the British Isles, it will provide enjoyment and pleasure whenever you use it.

TIP: If you have a cat, keep it away from the model railway, for the good of both the engine and the cat.

Some terminology

The world of model railways is probably even more confusing than the world of actual railways. Here are some helpful terms, helpfully explained.

Fiddle yard: A series of rails on which trains are held to be brought out in accordance with the schedule.

Dumb-bell scheme: A track layout with a loop at either end.

Scenic corner: A bit of free space between laid track and the corner of the room/table it's laid out on. Traditionally, you'd then put some model trees or a farmhouse or some plastic cows there, hence the name.

Out-and-back scheme: A layout with a station or terminus as its main feature.

Looped-Eight layout: A layout which looks, from above, like an eight that's been folded over, with one loop inside another. A very popular layout with model railway enthusiasts, as it manages to cram maximum track length into a small area.

A 'duck-under': A high baseboard which allows the operator to 'duck under' the track.

> *'It's your railway, and you can run anything you like on it. If anyone objects, you can ask him to leave, although it's as well to be polite; there's no need for both parties to be uncouth'*
> – C. J. FREEZER, *1001 MODEL RAILWAY QUESTIONS AND ANSWERS*

The Beer Bogie Bolster

Converting and rebuilding existing railway models for your own purposes – or 'hacking' them – is frowned upon by some model railway enthusiasts, but since you've just set up a model railway for the express purpose of ferrying drinks and snacks to and from, we'll assume you're not a purist.

One of the simplest and easiest 'hacks' for our Man Lab railway is to convert a flat-topped cargo truck into a safe, secure transport for a can or bottle of beer. Simply cut two supports for the bottle/can of your choice, taking care to get the circumference right, then glue them to the appropriate parts of your flat-bed truck, like so:

This will ensure that the bottle or can containing your favourite beverage doesn't roll, shake or – heaven forfend – tumble the three-and-a-half feet off the track to the cold, hard lino beneath.

Concrete Worktop

Research suggests that nowadays, the average British kitchen lasts for a mere five years before being replaced. Shockingly, that's less than the average lifespan of a goldfish. Or a ferret. (But not a mouse. They only live for three years.)

This terrible state of affairs is largely due to the rise of prefabricated, off-the-shelf kitchens that you buy off-site and are then put together in your house by someone else. In doing this, what modern men are basically saying about DIY is that they're quite happy to abdicate responsibility to somebody who's had a whole fortnight's kitchen-fitting training, just for the sake of a quiet life.

Pshaw and nonsense. You're going to learn how to build a solid concrete kitchen worktop (like the one we have in the actual Man Lab), and you're going to learn it NOW.

You Will Need
- Concrete • Cement mixer (or you can mix by hand)
- Wood (to make your mould) • Thick, tough stainless steel wire or reinforcing bars to build an internal frame for the unit
- Trowels, and a plasterer's float • Space • Patience

Building a mould

In order to make your Man Lab kitchen worktop mould, take a large, flat tough piece of marine ply or similar, and build your mould up from that.

The important thing to remember when building the mould is that the bits that will be indented in the concrete will be sticking out of your mould. In short – the holes stick up. Be especially careful to assemble the right-sized holes and recesses for the sink or sinks you're going to install (and, if you're being really swanky, a hob).

Your mould should be sturdy, but not so sturdy that taking it apart will damage the finished worksurface. We screwed our mould together,

and then unscrewed it later. Your finished mould should be watertight (obviously) and flat in the right places.

Once your mould is made, make an armature from the sturdy wire and/or reinforcing bars, to give the finished unit more strength and integrity. (We welded the armature together; however, you may simply wish to use a bit of binding wire – the sort of stuff you'd buy to use in your garden – to reinforce your sink unit's 'skeleton'.) Concrete is very stiff in compression but very weak in tension, which means that any thin bits (say, the surround for a sink) will be unworkably weak without proper internal support.

We varnished the wood after constructing the mould to make it watertight – wood will absorb lots of water from the concrete – and then brushed on some engine oil as a 'release agent' so that the finished unit would slip out of the mould with the minimum of fuss.

JAMES MAY

> **TIP:** Concrete will fray and crumble on sharp edges. In order to avoid this, use silicon sealant in the corners of your mould so that the finished worktop will have a chamfered edge.

> **TIP:** Since you're only using the mould once, you can simply dismantle it to get the worksurface out. If you plan on making more than one solid concrete worktop – perhaps to give one away as a wedding or anniversary gift – then make your mould with slanted sides so that the concrete comes out easily and the mould can be re-used.

The actual mould may take you some time to make, but that's OK. The longer you spend on your mould and its wire innards, the better the finished product will be. What does it need to do? Where does it need to be strongest? Where should the sink and draining board go? Do this at the planning stage, as any faults will be a bugger to rectify once you have to do it in solid concrete.

Pouring the concrete

Once your mould is ready, you can get on to the fun bit. Mix your concrete either by hand, or using a cement mixer (see 'How to mix concrete', p.193). Carefully and gradually pour into the mould, making sure the concrete visits and fills all parts of the mould as you go, using a trowel and a plasterer's float.

Leave the concrete to set for a long time. For the Man Lab kitchen worktop, we gave it four days. During that time, resist the temptation to keep checking on it. Have faith in the miracle of concrete. Slop will become stone, fluid will become solid and the potential will become the actual.

> **TIP:** Don't leave your concrete anywhere too hot, as it may dry too fast and develop cracks. Don't leave it outside, as animals may become stuck in it.

Once the concrete is finally dry, it's time to free your creation and show the world.

Removing the mould

One thing that will not have escaped your notice is that concrete is really heavy. Therefore, it's best to get two, three, or even four mates to give you a hand getting the mould off and the unit in position. Make sure they're all aware that it's a delicate operation, and the culmination of an entire four days' hard work. Promise them beer if that'll help.

Carefully unscrew all the mouldings and flip the worksurface over. You'll notice that there's now only one bit to remove – the bit that was the base of your mould, and gives the unit its flat surface.

Carefully remove the big board. If this part of the operation has gone to cock, it's back to step one.

Hurrah! It's all gone well, and it looks fantastic. You are now the proud owner of the Man Lab concrete kitchen worksurface. You may now bask in the satisfaction of a job well done.

> **TIP:** If you're mixing by hand, mix small amounts. Large amounts of concrete can be wrist-breakingly hard to mix and manage, and the mix won't be as good.

'Bliss was it, in that dawn, to be alive'
– WILLIAM WORDSWORTH, 'THE FRENCH REVOLUTION'

How to mix concrete

Concrete is a mix of cement, gravel, sand and water. So in order to mix concrete, you will need . . . those things. Acquire them.

Concrete mixing, like most DIY jobs, is a precise art that gets better with practice. There are numerous books and websites that go into great detail about the amounts of each ingredient, the amount of water used in mixing versus the amount of moisture already present in the ingredients, and various other pieces of scintillating concrete arcana. Please feel free to browse those sources if you feel inclined. For a quick fix, however, read on.

At its most basic, concrete is one part cement, two parts sand, and four parts gravel. This is the golden rule of concrete.

If you're mixing by hand, mix onto a mixing board or in a wheelbarrow, which you can then use to pour the concrete. Don't let the concrete set in the wheelbarrow, as it will then render your wheelbarrow useless. Although you may then win the Turner Prize.

Pour your measured amounts of sand and gravel onto your mixing board, and mix them. Make a crater in the middle of the resulting heap. Into the crater, add your cement, and mix together well and evenly. Make another heap of this, with another crater in the middle, and add some water, collapsing the crater into it and turning it with a shovel so it mixes well.

Use water sparingly, as the last thing you want to do is add too much water, rendering your concrete unusable. Add small amounts of water and mix until you arrive at the correct consistency.

When your cement is properly mixed, it should stay in a saggy pile when poured, but be soft enough for you to work with.

THE FASCINATING WORLD OF CONCRETE

You might well think that concrete is boring, but this is where you'd be oh-so-hopelessly wrong. We proudly present the unexpurgated story of the sexiest building material known to man.

Concrete

Conventional wisdom tells us that, like central heating and the sports stadium, concrete was invented by the Romans. But was it really? Even now, a fierce debate rages among archaeologists about whether concrete was employed in the construction of the pyramids. Some – most notably a French materials scientist named Joseph Davidovits – argue that the huge blocks of limestone are actually poured concrete, made on site, while others maintain that the limestone is natural and was simply dragged there by slaves (a resource that the Ancient Egyptians were not short of). See? I told you concrete was interesting. Barely a minute in, and we're already mired in controversy.

Either way, the name 'concrete' comes from the Latin *concretus*, meaning compact or condensed, and is – as I'm sure you're aware – the perfect passive participle of *concrescere*. (Incidentally, cement is also derived from the Latin *caementum*, meaning 'rough stone'.)

As concrete is all around us, and is largely used for building dull things like tower blocks and underpasses, we tend to forget that when it arrived it was a colossal technical innovation. It enabled the Romans to build incredible structures, the like of which had never been seen before on Earth. Perhaps the most famous of these is the dome of the Pantheon in Rome, which is made entirely of unsupported concrete and still stands today.

The Pantheon is a temple dedicated to all of the Roman gods (as the name suggests). The building itself is probably the best-preserved Roman temple in existence, and still has many rare features such as the original marbling on walls and floor.

As such, the Pantheon has been very influential on Western architecture, and buildings inspired by it include the reading room of the British Museum in London (now part of the Great Court) and the Capitol building in Washington. It's also rumoured that Wren drew inspiration from it for the Dome of St Paul's Cathedral.

Incredibly for such a staggeringly useful invention, the secret of concrete was largely lost after the decline of the Roman Empire. Some historians hold that Europe settled into 1,300 years of houses made of mud and straw and timber and dung until the breakthrough was made again, but this isn't quite true, and concrete was still used during that time, although not widely.

Concrete was rediscovered in 1756 by British engineer John Smeaton, who used hydraulic lime and an aggregate of pebbles and brick. Among John Smeaton's many other claims to fame are winning the Copley Medal for his research into waterwheels and windmills, designing the third Eddystone Lighthouse, and being mentioned by name in the Kaiser Chief's 2005 hit, 'I Predict a Riot' (Honestly). Leeds is massively important in the history of building materials for some reason – Joseph Aspedin, a bricklayer who also hailed from Leeds, holds the patent for Portland cement (1824).

The position of concrete as the world's number one building material is pretty secure – in fact, concrete is said to be the second most consumed material, after water, worldwide.

Despite concrete's long history, some architects would still argue that the Romans did it best – the dome of the Pantheon is still, to this day, the largest unsupported concrete dome ever built.

The three main types of concrete

Reinforced concrete – Basically, ordinary concrete reinforced with a steel bar (or bars). The statue of Christ the Redeemer in Rio de Janeiro is largely made of reinforced concrete, and – perhaps even more impressively – so is the Man Lab kitchen worktop covered elsewhere in this volume.

Pre-stressed concrete – As concrete is weak in tension, the concrete carries within it steel tendons, designed to combat this flaw, meaning that the concrete has a greater load-bearing capacity and therefore more structural applications. Most modern office blocks have pre-stressed concrete floors.

Precast concrete – Which is already pre-moulded into units before it arrives on the construction site.

Make a Fish-Finger Sandwich (FFS) ☑

Many modern people are dismissive of the fish finger, regarding it as a cheap convenience foodstuff for the unsophisticated. This is pure cant. The fish finger is a complete balanced diet helpfully presented in a portable finger format, and the sort of food humankind would take on the long, one-way voyage to Mars. Served in a sandwich, it offers the added benefit of being eatable with one hand, meaning the other one can be left caked in the grime of honest toil.

Apart from anything else, we owe it to those brave men and women who gave so much for us during the Cod War to eat the odd FFS.

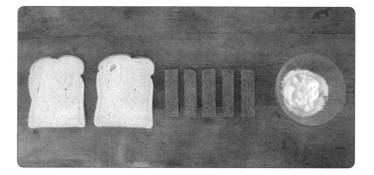

You Will Need

- **Fish fingers.** 5 x fish fingers is the required number for a proper fish-finger manwich
- **2 x slices of white bread.** It's important that the bread is stiff, for sandwich integrity
- **Garnish.** You can either buy some or make your own (see below).

Step by step:

- Fry your fish fingers in a drop of vegetable or olive oil. Five to six minutes per side will do it. You can also grill them, if you're some sort of dangerous health fanatic.

- While the fish fingers are frying, prepare your garnish. If you're doing this properly, you'll need to make your own sauce tartare (see the cryptically named 'Making your own sauce tartare', below). You can also use tomato ketchup, brown sauce or anything you fancy, really.

Making your own sauce tartare

Making sauce tartare – sometimes known as tartare sauce – can take ages and requires the tedious procurement of many ingredients, which is why we've got a quick and easy version you can whip up in no minutes flat. You'll need salad cream and sandwich spread.

- Pour a tablespoon of salad cream into a glass. Then add roughly the same amount of sandwich spread, and stir vigorously.

- And you're done.

Constructing your sandwich

After you've finished making your sauce tartare, your fish fingers should now be cooked. Ideally, they should be browned (read 'lightly burned') on both sides.

Using a pair of tongs, arrange the fish fingers (see left). You will note that five of them fit exactly onto a standard slice of bread. This is no accident – the fish finger was designed for exactly this purpose.

You should then cut your sandwich straight down the central width of the slice of bread.

That way, you'll have precisely two-and-a-half fish fingers in each half.

Mmmmm

You may now sit down and enjoy the fruits of your labours. You should realise at this point that if fish fingers had been invented 2,000 years ago, they would now be part of Holy Communion.

A Brief History of Fish Fingers

*I*F YOU CHOSE to travel the seas in an eighteenth-century galleon staffed solely by children while you ponced about dressed up as a sea captain, the United Nations would probably send a gunboat after you, and quite right too. Nonetheless, this is how one major supplier of fish fingers has traditionally advertised their wares, and it works – fish fingers are consumed in great numbers all over the world.

Fish fingers were created by Birds Eye in Great Yarmouth, in 1955. The slogan used to advertise them was 'No bones, no waste, no smell, no fuss', which gives you some idea of how low consumer expectations were back then – 'I don't have to behead and gut the fish myself, you say? A miracle!' 600 tons were sold in the first year alone.

Birds Eye Cod Fillet Fish Fingers have only 100% natural ingredients. No artificial colours or flavourings.

Americans have their own variety, fish sticks (not to be confused with 'crab sticks' – which, in turn, are not to be confused with anything that contains actual crab, because they don't). It's been claimed that fish sticks were invented as a way of selling more cod, when cod was incredibly plentiful and fishermen needed to shift tons of it. As cod becomes ever rarer, some fish fingers now contain pollock, haddock or even farmed salmon.

How to Tune a Guitar, and Serenade your Sweetheart

Just say there's someone you fancy in the office. What do you do about it? Quietly sit back and do nothing until Nigel from IT Support asks her out? Buy her some cheap chocolates and a boss-eyed teddy bear that says 'I ♥ You' on its flame-retardant belly? Mumblingly ask her for a pint in the Gotterdammerung and Firkin in the shopping arcade? No. You will do none of these things. You are a proper man, and you will go a-wooing in the proper manner.

With song.

Why should you serenade someone?

There are many reasons why you should consider serenading the object of your desires, but the main one, to me, is that most people would still be flattered to receive a genuine romantic gesture. In our postmodern, irony-soaked world, it's seen almost as a sign of weakness to be enthusiastic or genuine about anything. This is, of course, a very narrow and blinkered view, and means the part of the soul that enjoys the frivolous, daft, passionate things that make life worthwhile is secretly starved.

So, while the outward part of most people would feign sneering, ironic detachment at a heartfelt gesture like being serenaded, rest assured – another, far older and stronger part of someone is moved and touched.

And while they still think you're an idiot, they now think you're a brave, romantic idiot.

What have you got to lose?

I was a Teenage Minstrel

So why, pray, should you, the punter, defer to me, James Daniel May, on matters of minstrelsy? Well, I have a confession to make. I was a professional minstrel. In the 1970s, as a student, I worked in a 'themed' banqueting hall, adding atmosphere to the place as an actual minstrel. 'Twas my job to stroll around, lute in hand, in Elizabethan garb, serenading the punters. I did it for money.

The upshot of all this is that when it comes to wooing with song, I know whereof I speak, and am able to pass on all the tips I learned in my six months behind the lute, cowering behind an upturned table.

Easier than it Looks – Guaranteed

'I should have learned to play the guitar' laments the fat 1980s computer-graphics removal man in Dire Straits 'Money for Nothing' video. Well, maybe we all should, but the good news about serenading – and minstrelsy in general – is that you don't have to.

There's a very neat trick you can do that will prevent you from having to learn any actual chords. Some musicians will protest and harrumph and insist that this is cheating, and that you should learn the chords properly, but in your defence, you've got seducing to do, and therefore don't have time. Cheating will do.

Tuning to Perfect Open Fifths

(Of course, if you can already play the guitar, you can skip this bit. Unless you're feeling lazy.)

Normally, the six strings of a guitar are tuned to E, A, D, G, B and E, which makes playing the guitar an actual skill that you'd have to actually learn. But – there are ways to tune a guitar so that it sounds as if you know what you're doing! And the easiest way is to tune the guitar to 'open fifths'.

Using this 'open' method, the guitar is tuned so that when you pluck the six open strings they form a chord rather than a random collection of notes as per the standard tuning above. This allows the amateur to play without the need for all that complicated finger placement that takes so long to learn (and tends to involve your pinkie contorting in some unnatural and painful manner). Instead, you form chords by simply laying your index finger straight down the fretboard across all six strings – a technique known as 'barring'. This kind of tuning, which enables you to play without finger placing, is generally known as 'alternative tuning'.

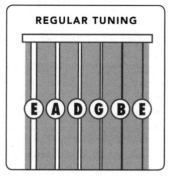

REGULAR TUNING

E A D G B E

How to tune to an open fifth

Now, normally these alternative tunings include what's known as the 'third', which is the note that gives a chord its Major (happy – think the intro to The Beatles' 'Here Comes the Sun') or Minor (dark – think the Rolling Stones' 'Paint it Black') tonality. But to get the 'perfect' tone to

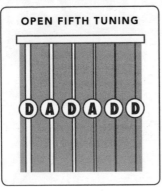

accompany your beautiful balladry, this tuning will include only the root note (C, D or G) and its fifth (G, A or D respectively) – which is why we call this 'open fifths'. In essence, you're creating the most basic guitar chord known to man: two notes played simultaneously.

If that sounds complicated, fear not – it really isn't. And to prove it, let's tune to D (which frankly is the simplest example). You'll need an electronic tuner.

1. Locate the first string of the guitar. It's the string nearest to your face when you're holding the guitar in playing position. It's also the thickest.
2. Pluck this string. As you do so, keep an eye on your electronic tuner to see what pitch the string is vibrating at. Most non-open fifth-tuned guitars will have this string tuned to low E. Loosen the tuning key on the machine head until the pitch becomes D.
3. Using the same method, tune the second string to A. (NB – it may already be tuned to A, as this matches the standard tuning).
4. Tune the third string to D. (Once again, you may not have to, as this also matches the standard tuning).
5. Tune the fourth string up to A.
6. Tune the fifth string up to D.
7. Tune the sixth string down to D.

And that's it. You'll notice that this has created a lot of A and D notes, but don't worry as that's fewer notes to clash with when you start singing. (The notes for tuning to open C and open G are different, so be sure to find out what they are if you want to attempt them.)

Once you've done this, you can – sort of – play any chord you like, simply by moving your 'barred' finger up and down the fretboard. However, for starters locate frets 5 and 7 (they should have a little round dot to help you identify them). Pluck the open strings. Then move up and bar the fifth and then the seventh frets. This is the basic 'three chord progression' that will form the perfect accompaniment to your ballad. It's also the basis of almost every rock and roll song you've ever heard. In short, you'll be amazed how competent you'll sound.

So – you've tuned your guitar, you've found out your sweetheart's address and you're ready to sing lustily to them from the street outside. There's only one important matter to be settled.

What to sing?

This is a potential minefield. Contemporary love songs tend to fall into one of four categories. They tend to be either:
a) Naff
b) Mechanical, and shorn of any genuine emotion
c) Good, but over-familiar to the point where they don't mean anything personal to anyone anymore
d) Written by James Blunt

> **TIP:** If all of the above looks too daunting, ask a mate who can play the guitar to help you. Explain that it's a matter of life and death.

> **TIP:** Another serenading cheat that we used on the Man Lab TV show was to Sellotape the lyrics of the song to the serenader's guitar. Try not to make this too obvious, otherwise you will undermine the carefully constructed image of yourself as a man of spontaneous passion.

Which renders all of them unfit for serenading. So forget the love songs of now.

You could of course pen a love song yourself, but there aren't enough pages in this book to make a list of the ways in which that could go wrong. Just type the words 'Love song I wrote' into YouTube, or 'My love poetry' into Google, if you don't believe me.

So we've ruled out the love songs of today and love songs you've written yourself. What does that leave us with? We need something both classic and classy, relevant to the now but utterly timeless.

There's only one man for the job.

Thomas Campion – the Tudor Barry White

Thomas Campion (1567–1620) was a prolific writer of ballads and songs designed to woo a lady. Between 1601 and 1617, Campion published four* *Books of Ayres*, containing lute songs, mostly tailored for the art of seduction, for which he wrote both the words and the music. Among the best known of his songs are 'Cherry Ripe', 'Laura' (not the one done by Scissor Sisters), 'Break Now My Heart and Die', and 'My Sweetest Lesbia' (the latter of which I suggest you don't sing).

Campion was very aware that music was a powerful tool for seduction, though one that had the capacity to expose the minstrel to exquisite heartbreak – or, to put it another way, when it came to pulling birds with a guitar, he'd been there, done that, and bought the jerkin. Lyrics such as the following give you a flavour of the Campion approach, and the risks it exposed the minstrel to:

> 'All that I sung still to her praise did tend;
> Still she was first, still she my songs did end;
> Yet she my love and music both doth fly,
> The music that her echo is and beauty's sympathy:
> Then let my notes pursue her scornful flight!
> It shall suffice that they were breathed and
> died for her delight'
> – THOMAS CAMPION, 'FOLLOW YOUR SAINT', A BOOK OF AYRES, 1601

What Campion's basically saying here is that although there's everything to play for, your hopes may yet be dashed. But then you already knew that.

> **TIP:** Get hold of a volume of Campion's love poems and songs and pick one that works for you. Learn to play it or at least strum along to it so it sounds like you know what you're doing.

A wandering minstrel: you

So, you have your guitar, tuned so deftly that it could now be played by a reasonably competent gibbon. You have some of the finest and most poignant declarations of love ever penned by an Englishman, albeit Sellotaped to your guitar. You have your sweetheart's home address, and a mate who's agreed to drive you there, and possibly console you afterwards should it all go pear-shaped.

Most important of all, you have a heart filled with love and lust, and the earnest desire to express it, in the direction of the one person who matters. So, what are you waiting for?

In summary:

1. Always sing Thomas Campion.
2. Tune your guitar to open fifths (see above).
3. Find out where she lives. In ways that will stand up to cross examination in court.
   Best of luck, good minstrel.

Top five Thomas Campion chat-up lines:

1. 'Heaven is music, and thy beauty's Birth is heavenly'. (From 'Laura')
2. 'There is a garden in her face, Where roses and white lilies blow; A heavenly paradise is that place, Wherein all pleasant fruits do flow'. (From 'Cherry Ripe')
3. 'The summer hath his joys, And winter his delights; Though love and all his pleasures are but toys, They shorten tedious nights'. (From 'Now Winter Nights Enlarge')
4. 'Come Trent and Humber and fair Thames; Dread ocean, haste with all thy streams,
   And if you cannot quench my fire, Oh, drown both me and my desire.' (From 'Fire, Fire, Fire!')
5. 'Thy fair face my wits and senses both have dulled; So get your coat, 'cos you have pulled.' (unsourced).

* Thomas Campion actually published five *Books of Ayres* – the first in 1601, which includes the aforementioned 'My Sweetest Lesbia', was penned in collaboration with his best friend and fellow romantic Philip Rossetter (1567–1623). Campion went on to publish *Two Books of Ayres* in 1613 (although there is some doubt about the exact date) and *The Third and Fourth Book of Ayres* in 1617, all of which were exclusively his own work. Thus, confusingly, Campion published five books of Ayres but chose to call the 'fourth' and 'fifth' the 'third' and 'fourth'. To Campion, collaborations don't count, obviously. It would be absolutely untrue to say that poetry scholars have debated this minor point of literary history for the past 400 years.

How to Polish Boots ✓

Nowadays, with every woman in the world owning nine pairs of knee-length leather boots, it's more important than ever to be able to set an example and demonstrate that we're able to properly look after a pair of boots – and are even capable of restoring a knackered pair to their former shine. Knowing how to polish a pair of stout leather boots is one of the fundamental man skills.

So, with that in mind, we're going to teach you how to polish a pair of boots so well that you'll be able to see the future in them.

> 'There's man all over for you, blaming
> on his boots the fault of his feet'
> – SAMUEL BECKETT, WAITING FOR GODOT

Boot polishing – why bother?

In the age of the trainer, it might strike us as odd and a bit archaic to polish boots and shoes to a brilliant shine, but even now it's a skill very definitely worth acquiring. Society still requires men to wear shiny shoes quite a lot in life – at weddings, job interviews, court appearances, etc. – and if you have to polish leather boots and shoes, you may as well learn to do it properly.

There are good psychological reasons to learn proper buffing techniques, too. Having a highly polished pair of boots is one of the requirements of any self-respecting army regiment, and with good reason. Boot-care says a lot about a soldier. If a man can take care of his boots, then it can be ascertained that he's probably fit to be in charge of a gun or a Challenger 2 battle tank. A polished pair of boots shows you are responsible and prepared; that you take tasks seriously and that you can take care of yourself.*

You Will Need

• A tin of boot polish • Two (yes, two) boot-brushes. An 'On' brush, for putting the polish on, and an 'Off' brush for . . . you're ahead of me • A soft cloth

---

* A man with shiny boots can be relied upon to take care of other things, too. When her husband returned from military service, Sarah Churchill, Duchess of Marlborough (1660–1744), famously recorded: 'The Duke returned from the wars today, and did pleasure me in his top-boots.'

You can buy proper boot-brushes from any good hardware shop. (They're also one of those items that you might already own, and have forgotten about, so check under the sink or in the cupboard under the stairs.)

Those boots were made for cleaning

Here's the most effective way of cleaning a pair of boots, as taught to me in the Man Lab by Platoon Sergeant Mark Buckingham.

- Using your 'On' brush, slap the polish on. You don't have to do it in a special way or anything; just get the polish on there, in generous helpings.
- Then – using your 'Off' brush – buff the polish off – but leave a layer on there. As the sergeant himself puts it, 'A common mistake that people make is to think they're actually shining the leather. What you need to do is build up a substantial layer of polish, and that's what becomes shiny.'
- Take your soft cloth and dampen it. Then, with the cloth over one finger, take a smudge of polish out of the tin, and work it in circles over the boot leather. Be careful though – if your circles are too big, you won't clean the boot properly, and if they're too small, you'll be there till doomsday.
- Repeat over a period of days until the boots shine.*
  And that's it. Clean, shiny boots are yours.

> **TIP:** Before polishing, always give your boots the once-over with a damp cloth to get rid of any grit or dirt that might scratch the leather.

> **TIP:** A 100% cotton cloth works best – not a duster, as these are often dyed, and the dye can interfere with the shining process. An old white T-shirt is ideal.

JAMES MAY

* In theory, anyway. I actually failed this particular task on the appropriate segment of the *Man Lab* TV show, as I didn't apply the polish correctly. Although I was spared any regimental punishments like spud-peeling duties, the platoon sergeant did call me 'weak'. Which hurt my feelings.

Build and Equip
Your Own Bar

The most shocking fact we stumbled on during the creation of Man Lab was one that struck right to the core of the human condition – namely that pubs in Britain are currently closing at the rate of 25 per week.

What kind of publess world are we building? Is there no space for the simple pint in this bland new Britain? Is there no rest or respite for the average bloke, no oasis of tranquillity where he might have a swift one?

There won't be for much longer. And rather than do something useless about it, like setting up an online petition, we decided that there really was only one rational course of action. We would build our own pub, right in the heart of the Man Lab.

And show you how to do the same.

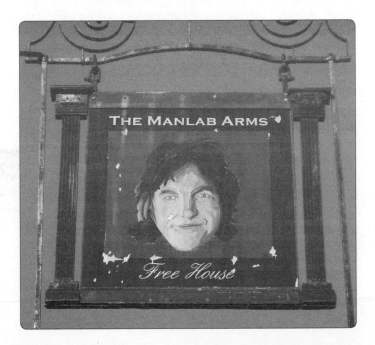

Building your own bar

As well as writing an article for the *Evening Standard* in which he pedantically set out the rules for making tea, George Orwell wrote another article for the same paper detailing the qualities his dream pub would possess. A traditional Victorian-style boozer with plenty of atmosphere, Orwell's pub was a place where it was never too loud, never too crowded, and the barmaid called everyone 'dear', irrespective of their age or sex. Orwell christened his fantasy boozer 'The Moon under Water'.

The fact that this name has subsequently been adopted simply as a convenient pub name by lots of different establishments (including one major pub chain) just shows how completely we in the early twenty-first century have misunderstood Orwell's ideas (see also *Big Brother*).

Nonetheless, we still have the power to turn Orwell's dream into a reality – by building our own bar at home.

A pub at home – living the dream

When they get the cash, the first thing many lottery winners do is have a bar built in their newly acquired mansion. And yet, here's you, attempting to live the dream without the vulgar trappings of extreme wealth, going it alone on an epic voyage of discovery. You're the Dame Ellen MacArthur of drinking.

Though it will require time and effort, the advantages of having a pub – or at least, the best part of one – in your own home will be manifestly obvious from the moment you start serving. For starters, you won't have to queue at the bar. Once at the bar, you won't be forced to make small talk with the barman or woman (unless you really want to). You won't have to shout over a TV inexplicably stuck at full volume on MTV because the landlord mistakenly believes it might bring in a younger crowd. You won't have to visit the most horrible lavatories in the world. The list goes on.

Most satisfyingly of all, however, you will – after the initial financial outlay of building and stocking the bar – spend far less on a night out/in.

Design and build your bar

But before that glorious day, we must concern ourselves with hard work, i.e., the actual building of the bar. You will need to give this some thought.

You Will Need

- Plywood or MDF for the bar top – or zinc, or marble or granite. Whatever you like, in fact, or can afford. Just make sure it's strong, and your bar is strong enough to support it
- Strong lengths of pine for the bar's 'carcass'. Two-by-four is useful for the uprights, with battening for strengthening
- Shelving material (could be wood or MDF – or even glass, if you're feeling classy).

STRUCTURE

You can design and build the bar any way you like, providing it has a smooth, flat, tough bar top; a sturdy, durable structure inside; shelves, for bottles, glasses, etc.; and space for additional features such as a keg. You'll have to put some thought into your design, but it'll be worth it in the long run.

When you're happy with your plans, rough out the skeleton of the bar using the two-by-four for uprights and the pine battening for additional strength. It's best to do this in square or rectangular units, and reinforce each rectangle or square with either diagonal struts or corner

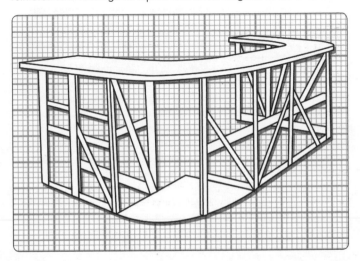

pieces. The structure should be robust enough to take the weight of the bar top, the weight of the bottles stored inside it, and the weight of fat people leaning on it and talking about football.

TIP: If you're having trouble getting the shelves in your bar level, please refer to the Man Lab Patent Adjustable Shelf Support Mechanism, at the end of this section.

TIP: If you want to get ambitious, the front of the bar can be curved. You can front the bar with plywood which you then screw into the uprights, and which can then be decorated with wallpaper or brushed steel or . . . anything you like really.

DECOR

Pub decor is one of those things that people have surprisingly strong opinions about. Some people like their pubs to be filled with rubbish antiques and engravings of thunderingly irrelevant things like the nave of Rochester Cathedral, or the Montgolfier Brothers' inaugural balloon flight of 1783, and view anything less than that as breaking the rules of the pub.

Fiddlesticks. Our Man Lab pub seeks to break away from the fuddy-duddy, and say no to such faux-Victorian nonsense. Our original brief was to build a 'groovy chaps' grotto in which the bell never tolls' – i.e.,

a bar you'd actually enjoy, rather than merely endure. So we went with shimmering stainless steel and designer flock wallpaper. You can of course decorate your bar any way you like – after all, it's your bar – but where's the fun in re-creating the local pub in your own home? Next thing you know, you'll be vandalising your own urinals. Make a pub as you'd want it to be, not as you'd expect it to be.

In addition to these basics, there are some optional extras you can add for a truly winning home bar. They include:

- Properly plumbed in pumps, drawing beer from a cask.
- Small behind-bar fridge/freezer for chilled beverages, ice cubes, etc. (so you'll need either a power supply or space for an extension cable)
- A small tray of nuts.

And there it is. You now own a bar. You are, at this point, permitted to punch the air and shout 'Yeeeeees!' in slow motion.

Plumbing in a cask

So – the bar is built, the wallpaper lines up, the shelves are all straight and your bespoke pub is a veritable haven of calm amid the general nonsense of the twenty-first century. Still, a few important issues remain unresolved.

The most pressing is how you will choose to serve beer at your new bar. There are two main options open to you. You could either:

- Serve cold beers from cans stored in the fridge (acceptable, but not very adventurous).
- Install some pumps and a cask, and hand-pull yourself and your mates a pint of proper ale.

To do the second option, you'll have to plumb in a cask. Let's presume you've got your keg and pumps already in place. You will now have to join one to the other.

Firstly you'll have to remove the buildup of excess pressure – which means whacking a wooden peg (called a spile) into the small plastic membrane on the side of the cask (which is now on the top with it lying on its side). So, using a rubber mallet, smartly and cleanly knock your peg in. Beer should fizzle out – but only the tiniest amount – and the great smell of ale should greet your nostrils. Ideally, you should then let the contents of the barrel settle for the next 24 hours. Tricky.

After 24 hours, knock your tap into the tap hole and plumb in your plastic pipes to the pumps. Or, if you've got no pumps, knock your tap in to the tap hole and lie on your back underneath it.

Test the pumps first by pulling a pint, and make sure everything's working OK and pumping evenly. Then pour yourself, and everyone else you've roped in to make your bar, a fresh pint of foamy beer.

> **TIP:** The spile must be removed occasionally to allow air in, to replace the beer you've drunk, but remember not to leave it out for too long. Over time, the beer left in the cask will eventually start to go off a bit, so it's best drunk pretty sharpish once it's all plumbed in. This makes a cask ideal for a party.

The Man Lab Patent Adjustable Shelf Support Mechanism

Say goodbye to uneven shelves with this handy shelf-levelling accessory.

You Will Need
- 2cm diameter dowel
- Screws • Spirit level

Cut the dowel into uniform lengths of about 1 cm depth. Then drill a hole a few millimetres off-centre in each piece, and drive a screw through it. Make sure that the hole is in roughly the right place on each fitting you make, though ultimately – due to the exceptionally clever way the Man Lab Adjustable Shelf Support Mechanism works – this doesn't actually matter too much, as they are fully adjustable.

Screw the fittings into the same height on all of the four uprights that will support your shelf, and place the shelf on them. Place the spirit level on your shelf.

Now, rotate the dowel under the screw (the screw will keep it in place) to adjust the height. Once you've achieved perfect flatness, Bob's your uncle.

JAMES MAY

215

Renaissance Man Lab

You may think that the Man Lab concept, designed as it is to explicitly address the decline of make-and-do skills in the modern man, is a recent invention. And of course, you'd be wrong. Tinkering in the shed and coming up with an inspired invention is an ancient and noble practice – pre-dating, in fact, the existence of the shed itself.

The golden age of blokedom in the western hemisphere begins during the reign of Elizabeth I. Under the auspices of Good Queen Bess, a variety of pursuits blossomed from quasi-magical hocus-pocus to genuine scientific breakthroughs, and the world was transformed by new developments in science, mathematics, navigation and design, which went hand-in-hand with new codes of honour and behaviour. The average Renaissance man may have worn tights for the entirety of his adult life but, nonetheless, he understood what it was to be a man.

It's therefore worth spending a little time examining some sixteenth and seventeenth century methods and practices. At the very least, it should teach us not to be scared of trial and error.

1. Navigation

'South till the butter melts – then west!'

– Traditional directions given to sailors attempting to reach the West Indies

One of the key areas that the Elizabethans excelled at was navigation. This was no accident. In the world that existed right up until the invention of the aeroplane and the jet engine, ships and boats were the most advanced exploratory vehicles there were, the lunar modules of their day. And in Europe, the rise of navigation was linked to military dominance and economic supremacy. Whoever controlled the seas controlled the world. No wonder Britain got good at it.

THE BASICS
Currently, in the digital age, we use satellite navigation to pinpoint exactly where we are and plot where we want to go. Before that, you'd

rely on your radio to talk to base, find out where on earth you were and how to get home. But these are both relatively new technologies. For thousands of years before all that, navigation was done on board ship and on land by measuring, by careful observation, by calculation and by a bit of trial and error. It was a proper skill, and people's lives depended on being able to do it well.

The importance of this can't really be underestimated. It's easy to be flippant about navigation in an era when a bossy plastic box tells you when to turn left, but for centuries, even apparently simple things like knowing how far west you had travelled were largely guesswork, and thousands of lives and hundreds of ships were lost as a result.

Matters of navigation were further complicated for the Elizabethans when you consider that science, occult magic and cheap conjuring tricks had yet to be disentangled into three separate things. Thus, the man who gave you sound advice about wind speed and the position of the Pole Star might also be the man who told you not to sneeze with your mouth open, lest the devil enter, or to pin bay leaves to your pillow on St Valentine's Eve to dream of your sweetheart.

Although some early navigation was just strange nonsense, those pioneering sailors and scientists laid down navigational techniques which are still valid to this day.

That said, navigating using one of the more dubious techniques might be more fun. So let's try that instead.

THE DOG AND THE POWDER OF SYMPATHY
Navigate the sixteenth and seventeenth century way – using magic. And a dog.

Thou Wilt Require
• 1 dog • 1 bag of 'Powder of Sympathy'
• A knife, or Susan Boyle CD

What do you mean you've no Powder of Sympathy lying round the house, nor the foggiest idea what it is or does? Tch.

Alright then, very quickly – Powder of Sympathy was a form of sympathetic magic invented by Rudolf Goclenius the younger, and brought to England by the Tudor scholar Robert Fludd. Its use was popularised some years later by Sir Kenelm Digby.

The idea was that if you applied the stuff to the weapon that had caused a wound, the wound would then heal, through magical means – a process known as 'sympathetic magic'. We moderns may scoff at this idea, but our forefathers certainly didn't, and Digby's book on the subject sold like hot cakes and was reprinted many times to meet demand.

What's this got to with navigation, you ask? Well, an anonymous pamphlet of 1687 put forward the idea that you could harness the miraculous power of the miraculous powder to tell the time at sea (and thus navigate) – simply by taking a wounded dog with you.

The method was simple, and – if you proceed from the principle that sympathetic magic is both real and practical – possesses a certain barmy logic.

Method:
Firstly, take a knife and injure your dog. Then, set sail with the dog, leaving the knife with a trusted servant. On the hour, the knife should be dipped into the powder, and due to the unique nature of the stuff, the dog – many miles away by now – will bark in pain.

Comparing the time in England to the time on board ship would mean that the ship's position could then be worked out (it's worth mentioning at this point that some historians believe the anonymous pamphleteer may not have been entirely serious in proposing this method).

If you don't want to wound a dog, there are alternatives. Indeed, when I attempted to navigate using this method, I did something only slightly less cruel to the dog, and played him 'I Dreamed a Dream' as sung by Susan Boyle. We then dipped the CD into the Powder of Sympathy later on, when I endeavoured to cross the English Channel.

In the event, the dog just barked a lot anyway, and whether he was trying to tell us something vital, in the way that Lassie used to when someone was trapped down a well, was unclear.

Thus, the results of the experiment were inconclusive.

But we rendered one Susan Boyle CD unplayable, so the experiment wasn't a total washout.

How to make Powder of Sympathy

If you don't have any Powder of Sympathy, you can simply purchase it from any large supermarket or – no, only kidding. You'll have to make your own.

To do this you'll need what the alchemists called 'Roman Vitriol' but we know better as copper sulphate. You'll need between six and eight ounces. According to the recipe in Sir Kenelm Digby's bestselling 1658 blockbuster, *A Late Discourse made in Solemne Assembly of Nobles and Learned Men at Montpellier in France, Touching the Cure of Wounds by the Powder of Sympathy*, you'll then need to beat it to dust in a mortar and pestle. Once that's done, simply put it through a fine sieve – but only when the sun enters Leo. Ask your local court astrologer for advice.

Once you have your powder, remember to keep it 'in the heat of the sun and dry by night' as Digby instructs, to maximise its potency.

2. Fortune-telling

As science and the occult had yet to part company at this time (though they'd do so fairly sharpish soon after, largely as a result of discoveries made during this era), many things were explored with a degree of seriousness that we might find excessive. Among these were the art of scrying, or fortune-telling.

The mathematician and occultist John Dee (and his medium, Edward Kelley), spent many years scrying in an attempt to gain the knowledge of the spirits, and make their fortune, with what can only be described as 'mixed results'. One of their scrying-glasses was a black mirror of obsidian, which, it was claimed, was Aztec in origin and was used in ritual worship. It's still on display at the British Museum.

See how far you get with your own scrying glass.

THE SCRYING GAME

Thou Wilt Require

- A flat black obsidian mirror made by the Aztecs and revered by them as a cult-object for many years before falling into the hands of you and your medium
- Failing that, use a crystal ball or any shiny surface which is partially reflective.

Method:

Stare into the scrying glass or crystal ball until your mind is clear and empty of all thoughts save the impressions you see in your 'show-stone'. After a while – presuming you don't nod off – impressions and visions will come to you as you stare into the glass.

Record these visions. Then marvel as they come to pass in the coming weeks or months, or they deliver unto you the secret of alchemy. Or simply rationalise it so you think that's what happened. The publishers of this book are not responsible for any misfortune that may arise as a result of communion with demons, devils or spirits. Or any conjunctivitis that may result after staring into the side of the kettle for two solid hours.

John Dee

No description of the spirit of Elizabethan enquiry, no matter how brief, is complete without at least one mention of Dr John Dee. Dee's entire life was a long enquiry into the nature of the universe, and his attempts to understand the laws of physics and nature eventually ruined him. Indeed, one less-than-charitable biographer stated that Dee 'cannot claim to rank among the world's successes' as he was one of those men who 'occupy themselves instinctively with the things which are too hard for them rather than those they could accomplish with ease and dignity'.

This is unfair; Dee made some calamitous decisions during his career, but he also perfectly embodies the spirit of experiment and enquiry that characterises the Elizabethan male – a man with one foot in the rational and another in the esoteric. Born in London in 1527 and educated at Chelmsford and Cambridge, Dee gave himself 'vehemently to study', and by the age of 20 had mastered many of the key disciplines of his age.

Thus began a short period of golden success for Dee – he became one of Queen Elizabeth's favourites, even setting, through astrological means, the date for her coronation. He advised her on navigational matters (which, as we've seen, were a big deal), and is credited with inventing the term 'British Empire'. Within a few short years, however, Dee's career stalled and he grew frustrated at his lack of progress. He began to wonder whether the occult – and particularly the art of crystal-gazing or 'scrying' – would give him a leg-up. If he could commune with spirits – and convince those spirits to tell him their secrets – he would surely enhance his own name, and that of England, and become rich into the bargain.

Dee turned out to be rubbish at scrying, however, and would probably have abandoned the idea altogether, had he not run into a man called Edward Kelley (or, sometimes, Edward Talbot). Kelley was suspiciously good at scrying, and soon he and Dee were filling notebooks with the results of their séances with spirits, all in the 'angelic language' of Enochian.

The jury's still out on whether Kelley was simply a con-man or not. On the one hand, Dee's notebooks – filled with messages in Enochian – seem to present a coherent and consistent language. On the other hand, some of the angelic instructions Kelley received are dubious at best – the most famous being from the Angel Uriel, who apparently suggested that Dee and Kelley swap wives, so Kelley got to sleep with Dee's comely young wife, Jane. Unsurprisingly, the two men parted company shortly after this incident, midway through a tour of Europe.

Dee's misfortunes piled up after this, and he returned to England to find his house at Mortlake had been ransacked by thieves, who had taken many of Dee's books and instruments. By the time the notoriously pious James I was on the throne, Dee had lost his royal patronage. He ended his days a sorry figure, looked after by his daughter and selling what few possessions they had left.

It's safe to say he didn't see that coming.

3. Food preservation

Francis Bacon, the Elizabethan scholar and writer, gave us many things – most notably the principles of scientific method itself. It can therefore be argued that Bacon is the founding father of science as we know it, but one of the inventions he receives the least credit for is his last – the invention of frozen food.

The story goes that on a snowy day in 1626, Bacon was travelling with friends from London to his Gorhambury estate, near St Albans. At Highgate Hill (the place, incidentally, where Dick Whittington is supposed to have 'turned again' and headed back to London), Bacon was seized with an idea. As snow and ice froze many things which then thawed out with no ill effects, might it not be possible to freeze foodstuffs in the same way, and consume them at a later date?

Bacon and chums wasted no time, purchasing a gutted chicken then and there from a nearby farmhouse. Bacon then stuffed it with snow. According to the writer John Aubrey, Bacon contracted pneumonia as a direct result of this, and later died, a martyr to the causes of science, reason and frozen food.

Some historians have pointed out that Aubrey's story is a tad suspect, especially when you consider that Bacon died in April, when it was unlikely to have been snowing. But nevertheless – applying a practical method to an everyday problem in this manner is clearly Man Labbing of the highest order.

FREEZE A CHICKEN – THE FRANCIS BACON WAY

Thou Wilt Require

- A plucked, unfrozen, gutted chicken carcass
- Some snow.

Stuff the body cavity of your chicken with hard, compacted snow. Then pack a thick layer of snow around the body of the bird (putting the chicken in a crate or box might facilitate this process). Leave chicken in its protective packing of frozen snow. Over the next few days/weeks, the snow will eventually thaw out, leaving the body of your chicken perfectly preserved (probably) and almost as good to eat as a fresh one (probably).

TIP: Try not to contract pneumonia and die during the packing process.

Conclusion

So, in order to ape the pioneers of reason's golden age, we've irreversibly traumatised a dog, let a dubious medium sleep with our comely wife and contracted fatal pneumonia as a result of stuffing a chicken with snow.

Overall, I think it's best to describe this experiment as 'a partial success'.

Other Prominent Elizabethan 'Partial Successes'

A golden age of discovery and invention also means a golden age of trial and error.

Sir Martin Frobisher

At great cost and risk, the explorer Martin Frobisher brought 1,350 tons of gold ore back to England from north-eastern Canada. Upon smelting of said ore, it turned out to be iron pyrites – fool's gold. The worthless ore was then used in road metalling. It wasn't all bad news for Frobisher though – Frobisher Bay in Canada was eventually named after him.

William Gilbert

Gilbert (or Gilberd) conducted ground-breaking early research into magnetism and electricity, the impact of which lasts to this day – a unit of magnetic potential was named 'the Gilbert', after him. Not quite so brilliantly, Gilbert believed that quartz was a form of water and that the dark patches on the moon were land and the light patches were oceans.

Robert Fludd

As well as bringing the Powder of Sympathy concept to Britain, Robert Fludd was also captivated by the idea of Perpetual Motion (something we now know is physically impossible, and contravenes either the First Law of Thermodynamics, or the Second Law of Thermodynamics, or both of them) and frittered away many hours designing perpetual motion machines. On the plus side, Fludd was the first person to describe the circulation of the blood.

ROBERTUS FLVDD.

Perpetval dreamer

JAMES MAY

Quick Tip

How to Build Flat-pack Furniture ✓

In times gone by, all you needed to do if you wanted some nice new furniture was to cut down six or seven trees, painstakingly hand-carve each required piece and put it together, a process that usually took about nine years. We, of course, live in the future, and although we're not quite travelling to work on jet packs or eating our dinner in pill form, we can at least buy furniture which assembles quickly and easily, with the minimum of fuss.

Or, at least, that's the idea you're sold when you buy it. In reality, assembling flat-pack furniture can be annoying, frustrating, boring, tiring and sometimes downright maddening.

We say: no more. Being oppressed by something designed to make your life easier is just silly. And so here's our rough guide to putting together all things flat-pack, even things with names like 'Bobby' and 'Roger'.

Check you have all the bits

Nothing's more frustrating than getting to the final stages of constructing something only to realise you're missing a vital bit. So check you've got everything first.

> **TIP:** The best time to check you've got all the right bits is when you're still in the shop. Considering most self-assembly furniture is sold at out-of-town megastores miles from anywhere, this could potentially save you hours of travelling back and forth for the sake of a single weirdly shaped screw.

To be fair, they do tell you to check the inventory in the manual. Which brings us to point two.

Read the manual

Boring, yes, but it'll save time and tears in the long run. At first glance, any self-assembly manual looks like an illustrated version of the Kama Sutra aimed at perverts with a penchant for half-built bookcases, but you need to get beyond that. Make sure you understand, in theory at least, every step of what you're being asked to do. That way, you're more likely to be able to actually do it when the time comes.

Bring Your Own Tools to the Party

Any self-respecting self-assembly kit will come with a tool or tools that will help you build your furniture. (This usually consists of a single Allen key and/or a toy spanner/screwdriver.) However, it might save time if you have the following tools to hand:

- Large flat-head screwdriver • Phillips-head screwdriver
- Power screwdriver • Ball-peen hammer
- Sandpaper • Spanners
- Your own set of Allen keys

MÅNLÄB

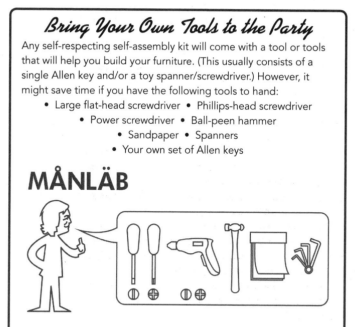

These should make the necessary screwing in and tapping of small, fiddly nails that bit easier. If the furniture is made of unfinished pine, you can use the sandpaper to take down any rough edges.

TIP: Go easy. There's a reason they give you such weedy tools to build your furniture – it's so you don't damage any of the crucial fixtures or fittings. They're erring on the side of caution. If you're using something with a bit more oomph, then do so with care.

Give yourself plenty of space (and time)

Einstein noted that space and time are the same thing viewed from different perspectives. He almost certainly wasn't talking about building a self-assembly coffee table when he made this observation, but nevertheless you'll find that your finished furniture will be better if you've got a free afternoon and a free room to yourself in which to assemble it.

Building flat-pack furniture, like so many other solitary male pursuits, is best done with no possibility of interruption, so you can do it as noisily, thoroughly and enthusiastically as you like.

Be patient

Flat-pack furniture is pretty flimsy, and you're more likely to damage it during the process of putting it together than at any other time. So be careful and be patient. Don't rush it; take your time (and all those other annoying, but true, clichés).

> **TIP:** Be especially careful with chipboard or any other 'engineered wood'. If you break them, they're extremely difficult to fix. Any cock-ups with wood, and you can usually go back a step and fix it with a wood adhesive. Chipboard isn't so forgiving.

And that's it. Best of luck, and remember: if you can spin the unforgiving rivet, hit sixty tacks and not your thumb, yours is the Earth and everything that's in it, and – what is more – you'll be a man, my son. Plus you'll have a magazine rack that won't fall to bits.

BogRoll
ALERT ≋ SYSTEM

Human beings have created rockets and put men on the moon. They've created the internal combustion engine, and left the horse and cart behind forever. And they've created the Internet, and put an end to the embarrassment of buying pornography from the newsagent.

You'd think that modern technology had solved every problem, large and small, in the modern world. And yet you'd be wrong. There's still no solution to one of the oldest and most annoying problems of all – running out of bog roll when you're on the throne.

We weren't going to take this sitting down.

You never think to look

Of course, the need to solve this problem wouldn't exist if you just checked whether there was enough bog roll before you'd sat down and started reading John Keats, but who does that? We live in a busy, confusing world. We can't be expected to remember every tiny thing. (The same excuse also absolves the person who used up the bog roll prior to you and failed to replace it.)

We need something attention-grabbing to inform us that there's no paper. Something loud.

Bog OFF

So, our task became clear – to devise some sort of switch system that would tell you when the bog roll dispenser was empty. A system that would recognise 'full bog roll' as OFF, and 'perilously few sheets left on bog roll' as ON. And would then alert you to the fact as soon as the seat went down.

I likened what I had in mind to the fuel warning light in your car – it would alert you to the folly of embarking on anything too ambitious when you weren't properly equipped. This was bold, radical stuff. We were pushing the science of bog roll dispensing technology further than it had ever been pushed before. Or maybe that should be pulling.

The Bog Roll Alert system

Thus, with our mission parameters clearly defined, we set about designing the ultimate 'bog roll deficiency solution' (to put it in contemporary management jargon).

Here's what we came up with:

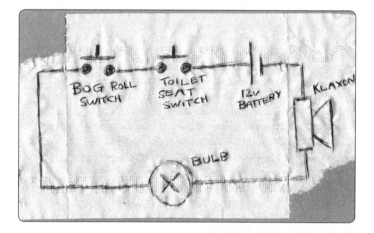

1. Two switches, one designed to activate when the quantity of paper falls to dangerously low levels, the other to sense the position of the seat. For the first, we used a long-lever switch with a lolly stick glued to it, to make it even longer, so that it could accommodate both an empty and full bog roll. The switch was set to activate when the paper ran low.

   The second switch was located on the side of the rim (basically stuck to the porcelain using double sided sticky tape) so that when the seat was in the down position it hit the top of this switch. Thus, the seat itself was the 'trigger' mechanism. If the seat is down and there is paper, you're golden. If the seat comes down and there's no paper, both switches are pressed, and the circuit is complete. A 12 volt battery supplies the switch, which then activates …

2. … a light and klaxon, which issues an audiovisual warning when a 'paper-deficiency scenario code red' is in effect. The rest of the household will then be apprised of your plight. (We suggest you stick to the simple 12v circuit option as in the diagram above. By keeping everything on one circuit and using a 12v bulb and klaxon, this avoids the need for a relay, and also means you don't have to play about with the mains current – bad when there's moisture around.

These switches can be 'normally open' (i.e. press to make the circuit) or 'normally closed' (press to break the circuit). For the bog roll sensor we used a 'normally closed' switch, meaning that while there was sufficient roll on the holder, the switch was held open and no power could pass through it. But once the paper level reached critical, the lack of tension on the lever closed the switch.

All you need do then, when the alarm goes off, is go and get a bog roll and re-stock the dispenser – or, if you've installed the Man Lab patent indoor railway, you can get someone to put it on that and send it to you, via the miracle of miniature rail.

What do you mean, you haven't built your miniature railway yet? Get to it.

Death on the Throne

History records no fewer than three kings who have died on the kludgie.

1. **King Wenceslaus III of Bohemia** was killed with a spear as he sat upon the garderobe – a primitive medieval water-closet – in August 1306. (Wenceslaus III, incidentally, is not to be confused with Good King Wenceslas, who was actually a Duke, and who lived 400 years earlier.)

2. **King George II** died on the bog, in October 1760. At the time of his bog-based expiry, he had reigned for 33 years and 125 days.

3. **Elvis Presley, the King of Rock and Roll**, famously expired on what he probably called 'the John' in 1977. The official cause of death was recorded as cardiac arrhythmia. The King's last words were reported to be 'OK, I won't,' in response to his then-girlfriend Ginger Alden's comment 'Don't fall asleep in there.' Technically, he didn't.

TIP: Exact figures vary wildly, but it's estimated that in your entire life, you'll spend between 1 and 4 years on the bog – easily enough time to read *War and Peace*, *Crime and Punishment* and *Ulysses*, so make sure your bog library is well stocked.

Beyond Bog Roll

FIVE OTHER PROBLEMS THAT TECHNOLOGY HAS CONSPICUOUSLY FAILED TO SOLVE:

1. **Death.** We thought that by the twenty-first century, we'd have achieved greatly enhanced longevity, if not actual immortality, by scientific means. Yet, despite many advances in medical science, the grim reaper is still well ahead in this particular game, and people still insist on dying all over the place.

2. **Language barriers.** It was predicted that one day we'd be able to speak to anyone else in the world simply by speaking into a communicator that would then translate our words, in real time, thus ushering in a Utopian era of world peace and harmony. A cursory glance at the news headlines will tell you that this has not yet happened.

3. **Living on the sea bed and harvesting food from it.** This was a staple of 1970s books about the future, which would inevitably have a two-page drawing of the domes and modules of our undersea home of the future, which would be faintly reminiscent of the gatefold sleeve of a Yes album. Needless to say, the sea bed stubbornly remains cheaper than prime real estate.

4. **Hovercars.** It was never really clear why hovercars would be any great improvement on cars with wheels, other than perhaps looking cooler on the drawing board. Which is where they've stayed.

5. **Android slaves**. Robotics has been the biggest disappointment of the future, and so far the most complicated robots on Earth aren't even as complex as a bee. However, breakthroughs in quantum computing – which vastly improve the speed and range of calculations artificial brains can do, which in turn means they might grow to rival and perhaps surpass us in intelligence – may yet make us wish we'd never bothered with robots in the first place.

JAMES MAY

HELICOPTER FLY CATCHER

Anyone who has ever been for a picnic will know that the basic ingredients are these: warm summer day, jam sandwiches, ginger beer, flies and wasps. Only the weather, sandwiches and ginger beer are optional.

It's time to fight back. There are many ways of evening the score – can of Raid, flame-thrower – but most of them are unsporting. It is fairer and more proper to meet the wasps and flies on common ground – or rather, not on the ground at all.

With this in mind, we set to work building devices capable of taking on the enemy on their own patch.

Gloucester, in Shakespeare's *King Lear*, famously observed that 'As flies to wanton boys, are we to the gods; they kill us for their sport.' So with that thought in mind, let's go after some bluebottles with the aid of some flypaper stuck to a toy helicopter.

You Will Need
- One or more remote-controlled helicopters
- Some flypaper

Simply attach the flypaper to the base of your helicopter and, using the remote control, steer the chopper round any suitable fly-infested areas.

Flypaper is available at any good hardware shop and is a gruesome, yet fascinating way to kill flies. It's not as popular about the house these days – for some reason, people aren't very keen on having a metre-long ribbon of adhesive paper dotted with twitching, dying flies hanging up in the kitchen – but for our purposes, it's absolutely perfect.

A radio-controlled toy helicopter, meanwhile, is something that any self-respecting bloke will either:
- have been hankering after for years (and has merely been waiting for a flimsy pretext like this in order to purchase), or
- already own.

Clearly, this is hardly the most efficient method of killing flies – but it *is* sporting. And it will turn what was previously a teeth-grinding summer annoyance into a competitive activity.

Wasps: Like flies, only worse

All of the above is fine when dealing with flies. Flies can't help their disgusting and disease-ridden nature. After all, they're curious, stupid and hungry, not malicious, bad-tempered and armed with a venomous sting, like their more annoying cousins – the wasps.

Waspocalypse Now

There are an estimated 195 million wasps in the UK. Don't believe me? Just try and eat a jam doughnut outdoors on a hot day. Most of them will turn up. It's virtually impossible to escape them, too, as they are persistent little buggers and like to follow you wherever you and your delicious sugary treat may roam. It's evident that combating the forces of wasp with conventional weapons would be futile.

Not being able to restrain ourselves from the natural urge to 'oversolve' the problem, we decided that the best way to end the striped menace would be to adapt our large powerful toy helicopter and arm it with several firework rockets.

The Patented Wasp-Destroying Helicopter Gunship

To make this fearsome beast, you will need:

- A powerful toy helicopter (we used the T-Rex 600 Nitro Pro, but feel free to choose a copter that suits you)
- Some rocket fireworks
- A battery-operated release system for the rockets
- A technically minded friend who will help you affix the rockets, and create and implement your firing system.

Of course, the problem with this approach is that it may render your picnic inedible by blowing it to pieces and scattering it far and wide. Plus, you may also not kill that many wasps. Or indeed, any. Truth be told, the above method is somewhat hit-and-miss.

But it is fun.

*'In order to save this picnic,
it was necessary to destroy it'*

TIP: Obvious safety disclaimer: never fire the rockets at anything that's not a wasp. If you do deploy the Wasp-Destroying Helicopter Gunship to attack wasps and, after you have fired your rockets, the wasps regroup and then viciously attack you, please do not write to us.

TIP: Wasps generally become more aggressive as summer goes on, and are generally at their lairiest between August and October. Bear this in mind when you are blowing them up with explosives.

So there we have it. Some might describe the methods listed above as 'overkill', but for sheer psychological gratification after years of fly-and-wasp-based torment, they are hard to beat.

Wasps – Hurgh! – What are they Good For?

Many insects benefit humanity. Bees make honey. Ladybirds eat aphids, and silkworms make silk. Wasps, however, don't seem to help anyone but other wasps, and even then, only grudgingly. What have wasps ever done for us?

- **They kill pests.** Almost every pest insect – an insect that's a threat to crops – has a corresponding wasp that preys on it or is parasitic upon it. These wasps may look quite different to your common black and yellow wasp but they're very important nonetheless. This makes wasps crucial in the natural control of pests, and saves farmers a great deal of time, effort and money.
- **They pollinate plants.** Most adult wasps eat nectar, which they get from flowers, which they then pollinate. (Admittedly, pollination happens accidentally, and they don't make honey or anything tasty with it.) In fact, wasps don't pollinate anywhere near as much as bees – Water figwort is one of the few examples of a plant that has evolved its flower shape to be pollinated by 'social' wasps rather than bees.
- **They help to get rid of rotten fruit and other waste.** Wasps are very good at getting rid of rubbish by either eating it or chewing it to a pulp and making a nest with it.
- **They inspired the plot of the film *Alien*.** The alien's parasitic reproductive cycle owes much to the life-cycle of the group known as spider wasps. These wasps anaesthetise large spiders and then lay their eggs in them. When the wasps hatch, they burst out of their still-living hosts, in very much the way the alien larva bursts out of John Hurt.

Know your enemy – Wasps and flies

The Common Wasp is the British wasp most likely to annoy you on a sunny day. The Common Housefly is the fly most likely to do the same. Understand more about these evil invertebrate bastards, with our handy cut-out-and-keep guide:

THE COMMON WASP

Scientific name: *Vespula vulgaris*
Active: April–October
Eats: Nectar, sugar, sugary things. However, wasps primarily prey on aphids for much of the season – their diet only starts to get sugary around August. This is because the nest-colonies are naturally coming to an end thus the wasps are out alone and no longer need to feed the larvae their aphid diet. When they're left to feed themselves, their diet changes to sugar. A bit like teenagers.

Lives in: A nest, with up to two thousand other Common Wasps, made up of larvae, workers, males and one single queen. The queen lays all the eggs, the males mate with the queen, and the workers find food for the larvae.

Spread: As a species, spreading rapidly into habitats and taking food away from more human-friendly species, such as bees. The Global Invasive Species Database names the wasp as one of its 'Top 100' invaders.

THE COMMON HOUSEFLY
Scientific name: *Musca domestica*
Active: All year, though they usually survive the winter as pupae (or as adults, hiding in your shed or loft). Individual houseflies only live for between twenty and thirty days.
Eats: Anything rank. Sputum, faeces, decaying matter, Scotch eggs, etc. Will also eat fresh and unspoiled food.

Lives: Everywhere. Flies can be found in all but the most extreme environments on Earth. Their global domination seems to be linked to the spread of humans, who provide the ideal conditions for them to flourish. They have an estimated flight-range of about 5 miles.

Disease: Due to their disgusting habits, flies have the potential to carry about a hundred different diseases, and as such have certainly contributed enormously to human deaths worldwide throughout history.

Five Ultra-Annoying Wasp Behaviours

- Appearing in droves the millisecond you open the first beer of summer
- Getting into your house, and then spending 45 minutes flying tantalisingly around the edge of a fully open window, but not actually flying through it, while you stand poised nearby with a rolled up newspaper, like a berk
- Falling into your pint as you sit in the beer garden. Then, after you've fished it out and it's dried off, drunkenly stinging you
- Flying around and around your head and face for no readily apparent reason
- Spending years quietly making a nest the size of a Shetland pony in your attic, which then costs hundreds of pounds to get safely removed.

REMEMBERING
NAMES
AT A PARTY

DICK

DELILAH

Outdoor bloke skills such as escaping from a category 'C' prison and predicting the weather by rigorous observation are but a small part of the skills that modern males have lost. Not content with allowing himself to become third-rate at manual tasks and DIY, today's bloke tends to be all at sea socially to boot.

This was not always the case. Not so very long ago men were abundantly capable of talking sincerely and interestingly to ladies, mixing a variety of alcoholic drinks to perfection and – perhaps most importantly – recalling the names of everyone they spoke to five seconds after they'd been introduced to them.

If you lack this last skill, fret not – we'll be rediscovering it forthwith.

Lovely to meet you . . . thingy

Perhaps you shouldn't be unduly embarrassed about not being able to remember the names of people you're introduced to at a party. Typically, what tends to happen at social gatherings is that the host will introduce you to 24 people *en masse*, usually within the first two minutes of you arriving, when you're still mentally shrugging off the rigours of your journey and finding out where to put your coat, your bottle of wine, etc. These are not the optimum conditions for remembering anything.

Trouble is, if it's a good party and well-attended, there'll never be a pause for you to properly get everyone's name, and that initial, rushed introduction may be all you ever get. Subsequently, you may find yourself talking to somebody with whom you get on like the proverbial house on fire, and it can be very embarrassing if you've totally failed to remember their name and then have to ask what it is – especially if they've not only remembered your name, but keep using it too.

This can be doubly embarrassing when meeting people you're anxious to impress (people who might be good work contacts, for example, or people you fancy). It can be frustrating for you and insulting to them for you both to reach a stage of mutual ease and friendliness, only for you to demolish it all – and put you both back at square one – by asking them again what their name is.

Meeting new people is stressful, especially if you're meeting a lot of them for the first time. In addition to introducing yourself and trying to be friendly and polite, you will be making assessments and judgements about the people you meet, and working out who you know that they know, and how they fit in socially, etc. There's so much you already have to do that it's no wonder that names get forgotten.

Well, no more. Using the following simple techniques, we're going to ensure that you never, ever forget anyone's name ever again.

Unless they're really boring, and you want to.

Getting to know you

There are several reliable methods for remembering people's names in social situations. Pick the one that works best for you.

1. Repetition

Probably the most simple method. In general, the more often you hear a name, the less likely you are to forget it, making this a crude but effective way of remembering it. Upon being introduced to someone, either repeat their name, or get them to repeat it, as many times as you can get away with without looking weird. If the person has an uncommon or unusual name,

ask them to spell it so you cement the name in your memory, and don't end up mispronouncing it. Break it down into syllables or visualise it as a neon sign if that'll help.

There are obvious drawbacks to this method – it takes longer than a normal introduction and involves you repeating a lot of names, which looks laboured. It also makes it obvious that you're trying hard to remember them all.

> **TIP:** Don't be tempted to make 'name jokes' as you make introductions – they tend to be tiresome and the subject will have heard all of them before. Also, relentlessly making a name joke for everyone will make you look like the kind of annoying wag whom most people cross the road to avoid. (Of course, that doesn't stop you making those jokes and associations internally if they'll help you remember.)

2. Physical contact

Making a physical connection to somebody makes them less abstract and helps you consider them as a real person rather than a name to be remembered, which in turn helps preserve their name in your memory. Shaking hands is the obvious one, though there's also kissing, a friendly touch on the shoulder, or even, as a last resort, hugging.

3. Word and image association

In her groundbreaking history of remembering stuff, *The Art of Memory*, Dame Frances Yates talks about how scholars from classical times onwards would build a memory system which they would then fill with strange and peculiar images representing everything they wished to remember. We haven't time for that, but we can attempt something similar on a smaller scale.

It's a funny thing, but the mind really is better at remembering details if they are strange and peculiar. One of the reasons we forget people's names at parties, is that mentally, we see the names – if at all – as being merely a list of words, making them much harder to recall.

This method means that you create an image in your mind that you associate with the person you are meeting. The reasoning behind this is that you'll then be able to recall that image and hence the person's name.

A good way of doing this is to imagine what the school bully might call the person you're being introduced to. If they're called Ruth, and they have buck teeth, think of them as 'Toothy Ruth'. If they're called Nick, and they're skinny, think of them as 'Toothpick Nick', and so on. Make sure your nickname is appropriate and easy to remember.

If you can picture them doing something, then even better. If the person you're introduced to is called Warren, imagine, as in the old joke, that he has fifty rabbits up his bum. The funnier and odder the image is, the more likely you are to remember it.

TIP: **NEVER address the person by the nickname you've mentally ascribed to them. Best not to even tell it to anybody. Ever.**

TIP: **The mind really is better at remembering the bizarre and unusual. The weirder and more outlandish something is, the more likely you are to remember it, which is why you can remember the face of Edward Munch's *The Scream* and the fact that Lady Gaga once wore a dress made out of ham, but you have difficulty recalling phone numbers or members of the shadow cabinet. The message is clear – if you really want to remember something, convert the details into a strange or bizarre image.**

JAMES MAY

4. Face association

A simpler and more direct version of the technique outlined above. In Face Association, you pick a unique feature of the person's face and mentally make a link between that and their name, like so:

Susan has blue eyes = the sky and sea are blue, and start with an S like Susan.

It doesn't matter how tenuous the link is – once it's made, it will be much harder to forget the person's name.

It helps if you can construct a little rhyme to help you remember, though this isn't always possible.

Susan, Sue, your eyes are blue/and that's how I'll remember you.

Or you can make it as simple as possible, combining image and name: **Sue/Blue.**

The more distinctive the feature and the stronger the link, the better your chances of remembering a name will be.

Method of Loci

'The order of the places will preserve the order of the things, and the images of the things will denote the things themselves, and we shall employ the places and images respectively as a wax writing-tablet and the letters written on it'
– CICERO, DE ORATORE

Without a doubt the fanciest way of remembering anything, the Method of Loci is an entire system of memory, and is the one favoured by professional memory men and women as a way of recalling complex information. We've already talked about Frances Yates' book *The Art of Memory*, and in that she describes at length the incredibly complicated systems of memory that scholars devised to remember stuff from the time of Cicero onwards.

The Method of Loci is so effective because it unites the facts you want to remember with a physical location you're already familiar with, giving the facts themselves an almost physical dimension, as they are now 'rooted' in space and time. The 'loci' you conjure up can range from simple mental 'trails' to the elaborate imaginary palaces and theatres of the Renaissance mind.

At its simplest, the Method of Loci involves you thinking of a place you know very well – your house, for instance, or a local park – and thinking of a route you'd normally take through it. Make sure the route is well known to you, and logical. Then, at key locations along the route, make associations with those locations using the things you want to remember, and visualise them actually being present there.

So – say you have to remember three names – Tom, Dick and Delilah. First you'd imagine your route – say the route from your front door to the kitchen – and then you'd place a name at each key location, like so:

Tom – Front Door
Dick – Hallway
Delilah – Kitchen Table

When you wanted to remember the names, you'd simply walk through your front door (in your mind, obviously) and go to the appropriate location, where the information would be retrievable in one form or another. It's down to you to make the image as arresting as possible.

The best and most effective way of doing this is to mentally 'weld' the image of the new person to a person you're already familiar with who has the same name. Picture the new person and the person you know doing something wild and outlandish together, and you'll be much more likely to remember them. It doesn't even have to be a real person – for example when you meet a Tom, you might picture him with Tom from *Tom and Jerry* with a knife and fork, smacking their lips as they carve up Jerry. Remember – bizarre and unusual images, welded to a strong reminder of that person's name, will make a person's name that much easier to remember.

Incidentally, the parts of the brain that aid you in this technique – the medial parietal cortex, the retrosplenial cortex and the right posterior hippocampus among them – are all involved in spatial learning. You're literally remembering where you put things in your own head.

> **TIP:** This technique is especially useful at dinner parties, and wedding receptions, where people tend to sit in the same place all evening, meaning that their locations can be used directly.

> **TIP:** The Method of Loci is extremely adaptable and can be used to remember many different things, such as shopping lists or phone numbers. Remember to use a location you know very well. This method seems very odd at first, but becomes much easier with practice. Remember – this is the method the professionals use, and they can use it to remember literally hundreds of things at once.

Locus focus

In some ways, the Method of Loci merely utilises what the brain does as a matter of course. Geographical locations tend to have strong image associations in the human mind anyway (this is best demonstrated by noting what images leap into your mind when someone says 'Trafalgar Square', 'Mount Rushmore', 'Wembley', 'Loch Ness' and so on).

Proof that the mind can combine fictional happenings with real places is abundant, too. If I were to say 'King Kong' and 'New York', you'd immediately think of a giant ape up the Empire State Building, something which has never actually happened and is entirely preposterous – but is so well known that the idea seems natural.

And there it is. You need never suffer from the embarrassment of forgetting names again. Although now, of course, your head will now be crammed with bizarre and unusual images.

Remember, remember

So – we've looked at a number of ways to cement someone's face in your memory. Let's take those ideas and make them into a proper working method, thus ensuring that you never forget anyone's name ever again.

1. Remember to remember. Considering how often we'll go to parties or social gatherings in our lives, we seldom reflect on the fact that we'll probably have to remember loads of people's names as soon as we get there. Before heading in through the door just pause for a moment and remind yourself that you are about to be thrust into a name-remembering situation. You can also use this time to get rid of any of the normal social anxiety that you might get from going to social events. As a result, you'll be more relaxed, and in a better state to not only meet people but also remember them afterwards.

2. Touch and repeat. When you are introduced to someone, shake their hand (if appropriate) and ask their name. See if you can repeat it back to them several times in conversation in the next few minutes. Remember, both contact and repetition work.

3. Don't fear unusual names. If someone has an unusual name, comment politely on it and ask about the name's derivation, meaning or origin if you can. Mentally, connect all the information together in as outlandish a way as possible (to maximise your chances of remembering it). Remember, any connections you can make will help you remember the person's name.

4. Use names you know to remember names you don't. If you know someone of the same name then picture new and old friend together doing something bizarre and weird and – above all – memorable. Connections between old and new as well as outlandish imagery will help you remember the person. If you're all out of ideas and can't think of any connection or people with the same or similar names, then as a last resort just imagine the person in a strange, bizarre and outlandish

situation and just engrave their name on their forehead, chest or even buttocks, depending on what imagery you have in your head.

5. Don't leave a forgotten name alone. If you do forget someone's name, sort it out as soon as you can. Here are a couple of strategies to minimise embarrassment:

   - Use self-deprecating humour: eg. 'I am great with names and faces, just not at the same time, I did faces the first time round – can I get your name again?'
   - Try the sly approach: Ask for the name and when they give it you respond with, 'No I meant your surname, you look a little like a friend and I wanted to know if you were related.'

   Both the above methods will almost certainly be obvious as a ploy, but they are polite and friendly, and make a virtue of awkwardness.

With practice, these techniques will hopefully become one smooth, simple process, meaning you'll never be at a loss to remember someone's name again.

Never Mind the Pollux

Cicero, in his *De Oratore*, tells the story of the birth of the Method of Loci. He tells of a sumptuous feast given by a nobleman called Scopas of Thessaly. During the banquet, the renowned poet Simonides of Ceos performed a lyric poem in honour of the heroic twins Castor and Pollux. Scopas apparently didn't think much of the poem, or Simonides himself, and told the poet he would only pay him half his fee for the performance. When Simonides objected, Scopas rather smugly suggested he redeem the other half of his fee from the twin gods whose virtues he had just spent the last hour extolling.

A short while later, a messenger arrived asking to see the still-sulking Simonides. The messenger told the poet that two young men were outside and wished to see him. Puzzled, Simonides went outside, but could find no trace of the young men.

Turning to go back inside the dining hall, Simonides heard a terrible crash – the roof of the dining hall had collapsed, killing everyone inside. The gods had indeed paid Simonides for his tribute, by sparing his life.

What's this got to do with the Method of Loci, you will undoubtedly be asking? Simonides, as the only survivor, was given the grisly task of identifying the bodies, something he was able to do with ease as he recalled where everyone was sitting in the dining hall. According to Cicero, Simonides subsequently realised that this method could be employed to remember not just the position of dead ingrates freshly smote by the gods, but anything at all.

the last word

In this book, we've covered many of the basics of assembling a decent toolkit – saws, planes, hammers, chisels and drills. Following the advice in those sections, you should be able to assemble a pretty keen basic toolkit.

But – and it's a big but – all of your hard work will be as naught if you continue to bodge away to your heart's content. Using tools properly is more than simply a matter of having the right kit. Without wishing to sound too much like Mr Miyagi, it's also a matter of discipline and attitude. Professionals don't rush a job, and neither should you. You should also take pride in your work and, as we've said elsewhere, set aside time and space in which to do it properly. Think ahead and plan, research what you're doing and make sure you know what you're undertaking. Make sure, also, that you have a plan B in case things go wrong: if a screw splits the wood you're working on, for instance, you should be confident that you can fix it with wood glue and clamps, or filler, or whatever's appropriate. Make sure you understand what the job entails.

There's also one other crucial matter that we've not yet covered, and a lot of men aren't comfortable talking about. That's right – size.

Measure for measure
'Measure twice; cut once'
– *Trad*

You can have all the fancy tools you like, but if you haven't measured up the job you're doing properly, then your work will be doomed from the off. That's why you'll also need a full battery of measuring equipment alongside your everyday tools.

You Will Need

TAPE MEASURE
Your flexible friend. A roll-up steel tape measure that stays rigid when you use it, but rolls up at speed into a handy pocket-size carry-anywhere plastic case, is one of the oft-overlooked miracles of our modern age. Before this, handymen made do with fold-away wooden rulers, which were much harder to get an accurate reading from and didn't wind up in a cool way when you put them away.

COMBINATION SQUARE

An incredibly useful device, consisting of a steel rule with a variety of adjustable and interchangeable heads. What makes the Combination Square the joiner's best friend is its incredible versatility – it can be used to perform a variety of measurements accurately and quickly, from marking out 45-degree and 90-degree angles, to determining the relative flatness of a surface. Most include a spirit level in the heads, but you should also get a proper . . .

SPIRIT LEVEL

Invented by a man with the delightful name of Melchisédech Thévenot (who also popularised the breast-stroke in his 1696 bestseller, *The Art of Swimming*), the spirit level is a cunning way to establish how horizontal or vertical something is. The modern design, created by Henry Ziemann in the 1920s, couldn't be simpler – a glass tube filled with coloured alcohol holds a bubble in suspension in the liquid. The tube is marked with two black lines. When the bubble rests evenly between these two lines, the plane being measured is flat (though of course you'll have to measure twice, the second measurement taken when the level is rotated 180 degrees, for the most accurate reading).

Another kind of spirit level is the bullseye level, which works on the same principle, but traps the bubble under a disc of glass, with a circle inscribed on it. When the bubble evenly occupies the circle, the surface should be flat on all planes.

TIP: Treat your spirit level with care and don't bash it around. The readings it gives will be much more accurate.

TRY SQUARE

Your own portable right-angle. One of the simplest measuring tools, it consists of a steel or brass measuring edge set at right angles into a rectangular piece of hardwood. You'll be surprised how often you end up using it.

TIP: Never mix up feet and metres, inches and centimetres, millimetres and eighths of an inch. It doesn't matter if you prefer to work in Imperial or Metric, whichever suits you – just don't mix them up.

MARKING GAUGE

A marking gauge is used for marking measurements onto the surface you're working with. It consists of a ruling edge, or beam, a movable block known as a headstock and a scribing device such as a pin or wheel. The headstock also has a locking screw on it which holds it in place while you mark. If you don't want to scratch the surface you're working on, some gauges can deploy a pencil instead of the pin.

Make sure you're familiar with all your measuring tools, and that you know how they work and what they do. This will save you time and general frustration in the long run.

The very last word

Detailed in this book are the bare bones of a good toolkit. You'll no doubt find that you use some tools more than others, and that you'll supplement your kit with useful odds and ends the more jobs you undertake. You'll make mistakes. You'll hit your thumb, perhaps more than once. You'll discover dazzling and colourful new ways to swear at inanimate objects.

But you've done it. What matters most here is that you've decided to have a go. You've decided to say no to years of sofa-bound inactivity and general man-apathy and claim your rightful place in the world as a Man Who Can.

Now get out there and fix something.

Glossary

6 – The number of teaspoonfuls per quart of water George Orwell reckoned made an ideal cup of tea.

Adductor Pollicis Muscles – The muscles between thumb and index finger, very handy for indicating when your steak is cooked.

Allen Key – L-shaped tool for tightening specialised nuts, usually hexagonal in cross section (see also Hex Key).

Backwards Walking – Technique which helps you throw pursuers off your trail if you've just escaped from a Category 'C' prison.

Bacon, Sir Francis – Inventor of frozen food, a cause he died for.

Ballast (electrical) – Device that limits the amount of current in a circuit. Not to be confused with:

Ballast (nautical) – Weight used in sail-boats to provide moment to resist the lateral forces on the sail.

Ballast (railway construction) – Crushed stone or gravel on which railway sleepers rest in railway construction. Good quality rock ballast is essential to track stability (we haven't really covered this in the book, but it's worth knowing).

Baseboard – Board that the track is affixed to in a model railway.

Bob – 1. Weight at the end of a pendulum. 2. Bloke's name, abbreviation of 'Robert'. 3. Hairstyle favoured by some female celebrities (and some Plantagenet kings).

Boilersuit – Alternative name for the Siren Suit.

Campion, Thomas – Pioneer of the ballad, and author of some of the finest love songs ever committed to parchment.

Cananites, Athenodoros – The original Greek ghostbuster, who acquired his reputation by successfully laying to rest the spirit of an old man in ancient Athens.

Carriage – The wire frame inside a toaster that the bread sits in.

Category 'C' prison – A prison for prisoners who cannot be trusted in open conditions but who are unlikely to try to escape.

Chamfer – A bevelled edge connecting two surfaces, usually at 45 degrees. (A square with chamfered edges would be an octagon.)

Crazy Golf – Variation of the popular old person's game 'golf', only with all the boring bits taken out. Also known as 'Miniature Golf' and 'Putt-Putt Golf'.

Crisis Apparition – A ghost that only appears at a time of great danger or significance. Or would do, if ghosts were real.

Crowley, Aleister – Occultist, magician and mountaineer, perhaps responsible for Churchill's famous 'V for Victory' gesture. Or perhaps not. (We didn't really cover this in the book).

Dee, John – Elizabethan astrologer whose discoveries led him to get an accomplice to consult demons via a 'scrying glass'. Said accomplice then promptly received a message telling Dee he should let the accomplice sleep with his comely wife.

Dew Point – The moment when moisture in a cloud condenses thickly enough to form rain.

EMF Detector – Device for detecting electromagnetic phenomena, which is handy for hunting ghosts – providing of course that ghosts are a) actually electromagnetic phenomena, and b) not made up.

Flex clamp Screws – Screws used to secure the flex inside a plug. This should always be done by clamping down the outer flex, not the insulated wires within.

Flooding – Trendy term for facing your fears.

Gnomon – The bit of a sundial that casts a shadow: any object used to tell the time in this way.

Hex Key – Another term for an Allen Key, beloved of flat-pack furniture manual writers.

'Horns' of the Moon – The points of the crescent of the waxing or waning moon.

Jasper – Slang term for the common wasp, origin unknown.

Kundalini – Type of yoga, possibly useful for controlling fear in any encounter with a ghost.

Method of Loci – An efficient system for remembering complex information, favoured by Mnemonists. Handy at parties.

Mnemonist – A professional memory champion.

'Off' Brush – Brush used to take boot polish off.

'On' Brush – Brush used to put boot polish on.

O-Ring – Rubber gasket common in modern taps.

Pantheon – Roman temple, in Rome. As its name suggests, it's dedicated to all of the Roman gods. Unlike most Roman buildings, it is very well preserved. The Pantheon's dome is made entirely of unsupported concrete.

Peening – Working the surface of a metal to enhance the properties of the material.

Polaris – The Pole Star, or North Star. As a result of having read this book, you should now be able to find this in the night sky of the northern hemisphere unassisted.

Powder of Sympathy – Renaissance hocus-pocus that gives you permission to torment dogs in the name of navigation.

Sauce Tartare – Tartare Sauce.

Scrying – Method of divination by which one might determine the future by seeing visions in a crystal ball or polished surface. Also handy if you want to invent an excuse to sleep with your friend's comely wife (see Dee, John).

Simonides of Ceos – Inventor of the Method of Loci, which came to him after his life was saved by the twin gods Castor and Pollux.

Siren Suit – Alternative name for the boilersuit.

Sole – The flat base of a woodworking plane.

Spile – A wooden peg used to tap a keg of beer.

Sprig – A small headless nail used to hold a window pane in place.

Tartare Sauce – Sauce Tartare.

Thrips – Tiny pests, the presence of which can seriously threaten one's man-garden. (Incredibly, this is not a euphemism.)

Ungentum Armarium – Alternative term for the Powder of Sympathy.

Virile – What you will become after reading this book.

Weapon Salve – Yet another alternative term for the Powder of Sympathy. (You can call it what you like, it still doesn't work.)

William 'Master Willie' McCrum – Inventor of the penalty kick.

Yoga – Physical and mental exercise regimen, utilised in the Man Lab for controlling fear.

Acknowledgements

The authors would like to thank all those who have helped in the preparation of this book, including (in no particular order):

Derek Jones, Editor, *Furniture & Cabinetmaking*, GMC Publications
Howard Andrews, Electrical and Mechanical Engineer
Sarah Darnell, Editor, *The Ghost Club* Journal
Professor Elaine Fox, Department of Psychology and Centre for Brain Science, University of Essex
Ben Smith, Secretary, Kundalini Yoga Teachers Association
Patrick Thomas, Surrey Clock Repair
Dr Andrew Stapley, Department of Chemical Engineering, Loughborough University
Helen Chivers, Senior Press Officer, the Met Office
Dr Alan Stewart, Columbia University
Dom Weir, Joiner
Nicole Day, House Steward, Chartwell House
Mark Gilchrist, Head Chef, Game for Everything
Tristan Gooley, www.naturalnavigator.com
Michael Nendick, Dartmoor National Parks Authority, www.dartmoor.npa.gov.uk
Dale Tandridge, ABC Glass and Glazing
Nick Morgan, Director, Sports Integrated
Deborah Rookes, Horticulturalist
David Cheek, Evans Cycles
Charles Ross, The Sebright Arms, Bethnal Green
Simon Kohler, Hornby
Dr Cyril Lynsdale, Department of Civil and Structural Engineering, University of Sheffield
Platoon Sergeant Mark Buckingham, Prince of Wales Royal Regiment
Dr William Kirk, School of Life Sciences, Keele University
Rintu Basu, Director, NLP Company
Max Andrews, Fact-checking Gibbon
Vic Moss
Will Daws
Tom White
Rupert Lancaster
Juliet Brightmore
Tara Gladden
Kate Miles
Laura Del Vescovo
Ana Zeferino-Birchall
Rebecca Magil
Bobby Birchall
Simon Ecob
Alex Morris
Stewart Batt
Sarah Christie
Alice Laurent
Emma Knight

JAMES MAY

Personal Notebook of General Usefulness

Useful biscuits:

anything except the pink wafers you get in the biscuit assortment tin,

which are the work of satan

Useful building suppliers:

Useful curry houses:

Useful exorcists:

~~Useful Fashion designers:~~

Useful glaziers:

Useful joiners:

Useful mechanics:

Useful model railway hobby shops:

Useful people:

~~J. clarkson~~

~~r. hammond~~

Useful penalty takers:

Useful sandwich recipes:

Useful non-sandwich recipes:

Useful plumbers:

Useful Powder of Sympathy shoppes:

bootes ye alchemist

Useful remote-controlled helicopter suppliers:

First published in Great Britain in 2011
by Hodder & Stoughton
An Hachette UK company

First published in paperback in 2012

1

A CIP catalogue record for this title is available from the British Library

Designed by Bobby Birchall, Bobby&Co
Illustrations by Simon Ecob and Alex Morris

ISBN 978 1 444 73632 8
Ebook ISBN 978 1 444 73633 5

Typeset in Avenir LT
Printed and bound by Clays Ltd, St Ives plc

Hodder & Stoughton policy is to use papers that are natural, renewable and recyclable products and made from wood grown in sustainable forests. The logging and manufacturing processes are expected to conform to the environmental regulations of the country of origin.

Hodder & Stoughton Ltd
338 Euston Road
London NW1 3BH

www.hodder.co.uk